Chandlers'
Travels

Chandlers' Travels

A tour of the life of
HARRY CHANDLER
packaged by
JOHN CARTER

Quiller Press
London

To Rene
Happy Birthday,
October 17th, 1985

1936 — 1986

Back cover:
Photo on Harry's desk is: Harry Chandler as courier
with his client Irene Ellis, later his wife, in 1937.

Published by Quiller Press Ltd.,
50 Albemarle Street,
London W1X 4BD

First published 1985
Copyright © 1985 John Carter.

Design by Kate Hughes-Stanton.

Design and production in association with
Book Production Consultants, 47 Norfolk Street, Cambridge.

Printed in England by Nene Litho and bound by Woolnough Bookbinders.

Contents

Foreword

S. R.

MINISTÉRIO DO COMÉRCIO E TURISMO

SECRETARIA DE ESTADO DO TURISMO

GABINETE DO SECRETÁRIO DE ESTADO

During the last quarter of a century, tourism to Portugal has made great progress and as far as British visitors are concerned the southern region of the Algarve has become their favourite destination. The success of the Algarve owes much to the efforts of Mr. Harry Chandler, who pioneered holidays there and remained a true friend of Portugal "through thick and thin" as the saying goes. His work, and the enthusiastic support of his wife Irene, has transformed the Algarve from Europe's best kept secret into the traveller's paradise. To Mr. and Mrs. Chandler, our warmest thanks.

The Secretary of State for Tourism, Portugal

– José Ferraz

1934–1985

1934

T HE PHOTOGRAPH hanging on his office wall was the last straw. The chief accountant knew that the clerks in the general office had probably put it there to 'take the rise' out of the junior, and perhaps even to get him into real trouble. But the sight of it made his blood boil.

Fiercely he snatched it down, holding it by its cheap passe-partout frame. It was a picture of the junior clerk himself, leaning proudly against his bicycle and grinning into the camera. Behind him was a sign in Gothic script – a German place name. He knew the lad had taken a cycling holiday to Germany that summer – dammit, all the office knew because he never stopped talking about it, showing his precious photographs and going over all the details of where he had been and what he had seen. Bumptious kid.

Kid. Yes, that was what made it rankle so much. Here he was, barely 21 years old, boasting of his travels on the Continent to an office of men twice his age who had never crossed the Channel in their lives. The chief accountant thought of his own annual summer holiday, two weeks in a Margate boarding house, the same as last year and many years before, but all that he could afford.

If he had analysed his feelings he might have made an allowance for envy – envy that he was no longer 21 years old and free to roam. But the office junior was a product of the East End back streets, earning just thirty shillings a week, whereas he was the chief accountant and office manager. He thought of his years of service, his responsibilities. It simply was not fair that this boy should cause so much resentment in the office.

The chief accountant crossed to his open door, stepping into the general office. The clerks looked up from their desks and ledgers, one or two of them half-grinning. They knew what was going on all right.

'Chandler,' he said brusquely, 'I wish to speak to you.' The boy followed him back into the small office, unaware of the reason for the summons and the sniggers behind his back. Probably expecting to be given some task or other, some errand to run. After all, he was the general dogsbody.

The chief accountant pointed to the photograph lying on his desk. 'Yours, I believe,' he said.

The boy picked it up. 'Thank you, sir,' he said. 'I was showing it to the others yesterday, but it disappeared. I thought I'd lost it. It's me, sir. At the top of the Brocken, sir. That's in Germany. In the Harz Mountains. It's the highest peak there, and I . . .'

'Are you intending, perhaps, to present this photograph to the nation?'

'Beg pardon, sir?'

'Chandler, take this picture away. If it is your private property, then keep it private. We have really had quite enough of your travels and your traveller's tales in this office. And I am in no need of a geography lesson. I don't know who you think you are, or just whom you are trying to impress. But I suggest that in future you keep your photographs and your stories for meetings of your East End cycle club. You have ideas above your station.'

He could see the sarcasm had bitten home, and dismissed the boy back to his work, listening to the jeers that greeted his reappearance in the general office.

'Let's hope that's the end of it.' he thought, pulling forward the ledger on which he had been working before his lunch break.

'Let's hope he gets this travelling nonsense out of his system and settles down. He's bright enough, and only needs to realise his limitations and his place in this firm. He could be a good chief clerk in ten years or so, if he puts his mind to it. But as long as he goes on with this foreign travel nonsense, he'll make nothing of himself.'

Cycling home to Canning Town that September evening, Harry Chandler bent his head against the first scuds of rain and recalled every detail of that encounter. Over and over again. He could feel again the sarcasm of the chief accountant, the sneers and ridicule of the other clerks. He was conscious, too, of the superiority they felt, living in 'posh' suburbs like Peckham and Wimbledon, not in the East End of London. The precious photograph weighed down his jacket pocket. His cheeks were wet with more than rain as he pumped the pedals. 'I'll show them,' he vowed to himself. 'I'll show them all that I'm a damned sight better than they think. One of these days, just wait, one day . . . one day . . .'

1984

The Vale do Lobo in the Algarve region of Portugal is one of the most expensive and exclusive developments in Europe. It boasts a five star hotel and its luxury villas and apartments are set discreetly among acres of pine, fig and almond trees. It has smart shops and restaurants and is built around three nine-hole golf courses designed by the legendary Henry Cotton.

As you play the last hole of the par-36 Orange course, you will see, on your right, one of the most luxurious of all the Vale do Lobo villas. Trekking up the slope towards the pin and the club house after your second – or maybe your third – shot, you pass right alongside its gleaming white walls. If you have a tendency to slice to the right, you might be tempted to pause beneath the pine trees and take a closer look at the place.

Automatic sprinklers wave lazily across the trim lawns and flower beds and splash the surface of the 30 feet long heated swimming pool. On the balcony – with its suberb views over the pine trees in the valley, towards the sea and the distant Monchique mountains – you may see a stocky man, dressed in casual shirt and shorts and wearing dark glasses against the bright sun.

Wave, and he will wave back, lifting a glass – or, more likely, a teacup – in salute. He has every reason to be friendly. After all, it is probably him that you paid for your holiday there.

Harry Chandler has come a long way since those cycle tours of Germany in the 1930s. A long way from being a thirty-bob-a-week dogsbody in a City office. It could be a million years and a million miles away. It is certainly a million pounds. And more. He did not give up 'the travel nonsense'. But despite having 'ideas above his station' he managed to make something of himself. . .

1985

So where do I come into all this? Well, apart from having known Harry Chandler for most of the twenty years and more that I have been writing about the holiday scene, my particular interest in him was roused when he telephoned me in the middle of 1984 and mentioned that his company – The Travel Club of Upminster – was approaching its golden anniversary. 'In 1986 it will be fifty years since I started,' he told me. 'And I want to do something to mark the occasion.'

The fact that he was talking to me indicated that he wanted to do something in writing, me being a journalist and all. What he had in mind, it seemed, was a special anniversary booklet tracing the history of The Travel Club. Something that could be sent out with his 1986 brochures. It seemed a reasonable enough idea, modest even, but the more I talked to Harry Chandler the more I realised that a slim booklet was not enough to do him justice. It would have told the story of his company right enough – charted its rise from very small beginnings in the manner of such things, mentioned the struggles of the post-war years and gone on to describe its present success. If that's all that was needed, a booklet would have been more than adequate. Even a booklet with some photographs in it.

But there is much more to the story of The Travel Club than a recitation of destinations and numbers carried. Much more than a timetable of events that can to some extent be parallelled by most other holiday companies. No, Harry Chandler *is* The Travel Club (and so, for that matter, is his indomitable wife Irene), so to tell the story of the company is to tell the story of these two people. And there is no way that the story of the

Chandlers can be confined into the pages of a slim booklet. No way.

'It'll have to be a book, Harry,' I told him. 'A proper book with lots of pages. Chapters, even. And it will have to be your story as much as the story of your company.'

So that is how *Chandlers' Travels* came into being. How this 'package tour' of one man's life and times and achievements came to be assembled. At one point I was tempted to look wider than The Travel Club and produce a history of the post-war holiday scene, because so much fascinating material has been gathered together in Harry's 'operations room' under the eaves of his Upminster home. But that will have to wait for some other time, for all that Harry Chandler has played an important role in that history. Many roles, in fact. That of goad and gadfly and catalyst for change, of prober and prodder into action of a lethargic establishment, even at times of the elder statesman and soother of ruffled egos. One thing is for sure, it has not been dull.

John Carter

PART 1

CHAPTER ONE

My Early Years

THE WORLD in general and London in particular, had many more important things than me to think about on the day I was born: April 20th, 1913. A Sunday.

While Bulgaria and Greece were squabbling over Macedonia, Lord Montagu of Beaulieu made a weekend speech about the need for aerial defences. There was controversy over the publication of the journals of Captain Scott – Scott of the Antarctic, whose death had become known only the previous month. And while Londoners grumbled about an increase in the LCC Education Rate, the good citizens of Crewe basked in the honour of a royal visit. Everyone was talking about the Cup Final which had been played at Crystal Palace the day before. Aston Villa had beaten Sunderland by 1–0.

As I say, there was plenty going on when I made my entrance in the small bedroom of a terraced house in Hermit Road, Canning Town, E16, part of London usually known as the "East End". I was the first child born to Harry and Ellen Chandler and the event was good cause for celebration. Nothing elaborate mind you, just a few pints and a bit of a knees up with one or two of the neighbours in true East End style.

On the very same day, in Vienna, a house-painter was celebrating his 24th birthday, although in fact he didn't have much to celebrate. A failure as an artist, he left Vienna a couple of weeks later and went to Munich to try his hand at something else. Though nobody knew it at the time, he was to have an important influence on our family and our neighbours. And thousands more in the East End, come to that. His name was Mr. Schicklegruber, alias Adolf Hitler.

My father had been in the army for most of his life. He came from a family of dockers in Bermondsey, joined up as a lad, and eventually went to South Africa to fight in the Boer War. The stories he told me were all about that war and he never tired of recounting his adventures to me and to my brothers and sister – brother Bill was born next, then came Olive and, after her, Arthur. I shall tell you more about them later.

The story I liked best was the one about the silver watch that he had bought for his 21st birthday in the year 1900. He had sent 25 shillings home to his mother and she had got it for him from Samuels the jewellers in Stratford-by-Bow. It went through the Boer War with him, from one battlefield to another, and 'never lost a single minute'. He would say that proudly, dangling the watch in front of us on its long chain. He wore it all his life and left it to me when he died. I have it still. And it still goes.

It is odd how things like that stick in your memory while big and important events make no impact on your childhood. I was too young to know anything about the First World War, but I can remember a lot of local excitement when a military balloon came down near our house. There was much shouting and running around, a rope was thrown down and some men got together to pull the balloon down into the school playground. I think my father was one of the men, because he was by then too old to serve in the army.

He ran a small shop in Hermit Road – the usual sort of grocer and tobacconist outfit – and another of my memories is what happened when he had a delivery of what they called 'ship's dripping'. As far as I know – and perhaps it is better not to know too much – this consisted of all the bits of meat and fat left over from the cargo (or maybe the galley) when a ship docked in London at the end of a voyage.

My father would heat up the copper boiler in the scullery and boil up the whole brew, adding a bit of salt, and letting it cool into a tasty kind of spread. He would sell this in the shop because food was scarce, and it seemed to be very popular. I think most customers preferred not to know how it was 'created'.

He would also buy up a side of bacon and carve it into joints and slices, cooking some of it on the gas stove. When I was very young, getting under his feet as usual, I pulled down one of the pans and the entire stove fell over on me. The iron handle of the gas oven hit me on the ear, breaking a bone, and I had trouble with that ear for years afterwards.

When I was still fairly young we moved from Hermit Road and took over another little shop in Stephen's Road, up in West Ham. It was not a good move because my father simply could not make it pay. In the 1920s and early 1930s there was record unemployment, over 4 millions, including all our neighbours – and this was a very poor area. I have never claimed to be a barefoot urchin, but I certainly did go to school with kids who had no shoes. It was quite commonplace in those days.

Like everybody else, my father was always scraping hard for money to keep going, but unlike many others, I was never short of food because I could always help myself to a handful of biscuits when I went through the shop on the way out to school.

Because of the unemployement and the hardships, West Ham Council used to dole out food coupons to families who did not have enough to live on because the husband was unemployed. They would bring the food coupons into the shop and the idea was that in due course, my father would get the money from the Council. The trouble was that people would run out of both coupons and money and would ask for credit against their next allocation from the Council. Once that started, the coupons could not keep pace with the money that was owed.

Of course, I could not understand all this at the time, but I was aware that my father was going through a difficult patch. From a business point of view he made all the wrong decisions, but he had a lot of compassion and these people were not just customers but neighbours. In the end he owed money to one of the wholesalers – a company called Bedwells, I think, which took over the shop in lieu of the debt. It was not a good deal as far as he was concerned, because I think he could have sold the shop and got enough to pay the debt and still have had something left over for the family. As it was, he managed to scrape together £100 and bought a corner sweetshop back in Hermit Road. He managed to make a living out of that until the war came along.

But I'm running ahead of myself. The war was a long way off during my early years, and a lot was to happen to me and the family before then.

As a kid I got up to the usual sorts of mischief, but nothing too bad. One or two of my friends went to Borstal and the rest of us thought that was very adventurous. I remember asking them what it was like, but they never told me, and I had no inclination to find out first hand.

My school was the normal mixed infants and juniors place, and I must have been reasonably bright because they put me in for a scholarship when I was 11 years old. I knew that if I passed really well I would get to the grammar school, but I was told that if I passed with average marks I would go to the 'High Lemon Tree'. I did not know what this meant, but as everybody was talking about it, I decided that the 'High Lemon Tree' might be an interesting sort of place. I managed to get through the exam and received a letter telling me that, although I was not going to the grammar school, I had a place at the Higher Elementary School. And that was when I discovered what the 'High Lemon Tree' meant: Higher Elementary translated by the broad Cockney dialect of the district.

I went there until I was 15 years old. Old enough to leave and start earning a living, although I had already had plenty of experience of earning money by odd jobbing.

First, though, my grand debut into the world of full-time employment – into the City of London, bright with promise for an enterprising lad. And 15-years-old Harry Chandler was certainly set to make his mark. It was July, 1928, and my employer was a company called Continental Express, a freight forwarding agency. The office was in Bucklersbury, which runs from Queen Victoria Street to Poultry, near the Mansion House. I was a junior clerk – in other words, the office boy and general dogsbody – at £1 a week.

Believe it or not, it was the first time I had been to the 'real' London, for the East End was a very different world and one you didn't easily

1920: *In the east end of London in the 1920's the kids played in the streets.*
Harry Chandler learns early in life to look at the camera.

1926: *Armoured cars in the East India Dock Road during the general strike.*

1928: *North Wales, my first venture outside London.*

1929: *Our first cycling adventure, camping at Bagshot. We accidentally set fire to several miles of the Heath, leading to my first brush with the law.*

leave. But there I was on that first day, all raring to go. I had been in the office for no more than five minutes before I was given a cheque for several thousand pounds and told to deliver it to an office at London Bridge Station. I could not imagine that this piece of paper could be worth such a staggering sum – it was the first cheque I had seen – but I discovered later it was the monthly freight account payment to the railway company. As is usually the case, they had waited until the last moment before dealing with the bill, and had got a telephone call from London Bridge chasing up the money owed. So they had agreed to send it over right away by trusted messenger – me.

Can you imagine it? Giving a valuable cheque to a brand new lad who did not know his Eros from his Aldgate and sending him off into the unknown. The only instruction I was given was to get on a bus which had 'London Bridge' on the front.

I let three buses go past the stop because I thought they were going to a place called 'London Bog' and I did not want to come to a sticky end. I had never known that there was a bog in London, but then I realised that the indicator board actually said 'London Bdg'. After that bad start I managed to find the station, deliver the cheque and take a bus back to where I had begun my journey. When I got back to the City, though, I could not find Bucklersbury and, as I had forgotten the name – it was only a narrow alley anyway – I could not ask for directions. I was saved by seeing a horse and cart coming down the street with 'Continental Express' on the side. I waved it down and asked the driver where the office was.

'It's in Golden Lane, lad. That's where I'm going.'

'No,' I relied. 'There's an office near here. I work there.'

He shook his head very emphatically and, when I told him I had only started that day, he said that I had made a mistake, but he would give me a lift back to Golden Lane. That is just what he did and I turned up at the company's head office, knowing I was in the wrong place but confused. One of the office clerks explained that I had been working in the company's travel office, and he showed me the way back to Bucklersbury.

The office manager was more anxious than angry. He probably thought that I had absconded with the cheque and that they would stop it out of his wages! 'You left here at nine o'clock this morning and it's now well after two,' he said. 'Where the devil have you been?'

I was too frightened to tell him about catching a bus to London Bog and going to Golden Lane. But it was a memorable first day at work. And I had discovered that I was employed in the travel office. I felt it was significant – but I did not know why.

What I did know was that I wanted to travel and, in order to do so, I would have to have money. More than I could save from my £1-a-week wage. So I set about earning more. It was not a new experience for me because, even before leaving school, I had tried to pick up a few shillings doing odd jobs at weekends. The first way I found of making money was sticking silver balls on wedding cakes. My father had a friend who ran a baker's shop and had a popular line in wedding cakes. On Sunday afternoons I used to go to the bakery and stick all the silver balls on the cakes. It was a fiddly job, but it earned me a shilling for the afternoon, which was a lot for an 11-year-old.

About the same time I started making electric bells for shops – my father's shop, this other fellow's bakery and all the shops down the street and in the neighbourhood. The device I used was known as the Leclanche Cell and was a very early form of battery — invented, I supposed, by a Frenchman named Leclanche. I fixed a piece of metal on the door which connected with another piece on the door frame. When the door opened, it made the contact and rang the bell. Good old Monsieur Leclanche. His invention earned me a few more shillings.

I delivered goods for my father on Sundays, taking the grocery orders to the local pubs, and I also had a stall outside the shop from eight in the morning until eight in the evening on Saturdays. From the stall I sold bread and cakes, rolls and pastries, and he paid me sixpence in the pound. On a good day I sold about £4 worth, so that was another couple of bob in my pocket. The only trouble was that late in the evening when the shop was closed and after we had cleaned up, I would go over to Stratford to the eel and pie shop and squander the whole two shillings. A whole day's work eaten up in half an hour, but what a delight. I like stewed eels and I had an enormous appetite.

On Thursday afternoons, after school, I worked in the shop, weighing the sugar from hundredweight sacks into one pound blue bags, packing it down and folding and twisting the tops over. Boring, but worth sixpence.

Looking back on those times, I do not think that I was driven to make money – it was not an obsession or anything like that – but I could not pass up any chance of earning a few pennies. I recall one Bank Holiday when I went to Loughton with my friend Albert, because there was a fair on. There was a big pond nearby, with clumps of bullrushes in the middle of it, so we waded out, picked the bullrushes and stood by the side of the road leading to the fair, offering them to passers by at a penny each. The fellows bought them for their girls, because they were in a good mood, probably a little bit drunk and feeling sorry for a couple of bedraggled urchins.

It was much much later that I learned that you could make money without actually working, but I shall tell you about that in due course.

Back at the Continental Express office I continued my money earning exploits. I volunteered to be post boy, running around and buying the stamps and working all the overtime I could get – from 9 a.m. to 9 p.m. – so I could buy a bike. The overtime rate was a shilling an hour, which was not much but was at least an improvement on my pay as a wedding cake decorator! I worked 120 hours overtime and saved every shilling so at last I was able to buy a brand new cycle from Gamages. Six pounds it cost, and I paid for it with a bag of shillings. I had not had it two months before it was stolen from the garage in Lower Thames Street where I used to leave it. But by then it had saved me a lot of money.

I rode it to and from work and saved the bus and tube fares – that was 5 shillings a week. I also rode it between the office and Victoria Station, delivering documents for the firm – and claiming the bus fares from petty cash, another 5 bob!

I suppose that was wrong of me, but while I am in a confessing mood, I shall tell you about another little trick I worked after the bike was stolen. On the trips to Victoria I used to go on the number 15 bus, boarding it at the Bank and going upstairs, sitting as far as possible at the front. This would be the last seat the conductor came to and, when he got to me, I would give him the penny and ask for Aldgate. Naturally he would tell me I was travelling in the wrong direction. 'But they told me to get a number 15 bus,' I would say. And, every time, the conductor would explain that I had got on the right bus, but was travelling in the wrong direction. So I would get off without having paid my penny, and wait for another bus so I could work the same trick. That way I got all the way to Victoria for nothing and, of course, I would do the same thing on the return journey, this time asking for Victoria.

Yes, I know it was cheating but, when you live in the East End of London and see poverty all around, you do not think it is very bad to cheat the bus company out of a few coppers. Especially when your bike's been stolen and the police don't want to know.

Anyway, this lasted only until I was able to save up six pounds for another bicycle and took up cycling with enthusiasm. It was my only way of escaping from the East End, of getting right away from London and discovering other parts of the country. Until then I had only been able to get away as a small child, thanks to the Country Holiday Fund, a charity that existed to take East End children on holidays. I remember going to Virginia Water and staying with an old lady who had a son of about my age. She used to take children in for £1 a week from the fund and as far as I can remember, you had to contribute, if you could, according to your father's income. My father chipped in ten shillings, I think. And that was the only holiday I had – a load of East End kids going into the country in a bus to be farmed out for a week of fresh air. A sort of evacuation in miniature.

With my new bike, I tackled cycling with great enthusiasm, joining the YMCA and setting off for somewhere new every weekend. At that time – in the early 1930s – it was the thing to do. There was a tremendous enthusiasm for cycling and hiking, with cycle clubs springing up all over the country. I recall the *Daily Herald* started a hiking club – which was a darned sight more sensible way of identifying with its readers than the bingo games of today. *I'm Happy When I'm Hiking* was a popular song of the time, and that said it all.

We would go off in groups of 20 or 30, aiming to do around 100 miles every Sunday, and make for Clacton or Brighton or somewhere along the coast.

What I was doing, in fact, was resurrecting a schoolboy enthusiasm, because I had actually had my first bike when I was around 13 years old.

I had always had a desire to travel around and get away from the East End. As I had no money, the only way to go was by bike. It carried me around Britain, up as far as Scotland and into Wales and Cornwall. I travelled all over those places at weekends and in the holidays when I was still at school. My best friend then, and for many years, was a chap called Albert Goring. We were at school together, joined the same cycle club, and used to go out together on our bikes. On Wednesday evenings we would go off to Brentwood to play billiards. That was a long ride from Canning Town and it took us an hour and a half each way to cover the 15 miles.

Then on Sundays we would go on more ambitious rides, to Bishop's Stortford, Colchester and Chelmsford. Sometimes we would venture to the other side of London – Margate and Tunbridge Wells, Windsor and places like that. Two or three times each summer we would go on a night ride to destinations such as Clacton or Winchester, Ross-on-Wye or Stratford-on-Avon.

We would set out on a Saturday evening and ride all night, stopping to sleep at the side of the road for an hour or two at about six or seven in the morning, and then continuing to our destination. We took sandwiches, saw the sights, and cycled back home, arriving around midnight on Sunday. It was a remarkably cheap way of getting around, cheaper, even, than the 'bargains' offered by package tour companies today. But I do not think the young people who set off with their backpacks to explore the Greek islands, or wander around Europe, would care to cycle all the way or sleep on the side of the road – much less take sandwiches!

When Albert and I went on proper holidays, we used to go camping, covering a tremendous amount of the country in a couple of weeks. We would think nothing of going all around Wales, then up to the Lake District and down to Cornwall and Devon. And here again is one of those little incidents that has stuck in my memory down the years.

We had pitched our tent in a field miles from anywhere and were settling down to enjoy the peaceful countryside when another camper turned up on his bike. He did not approach us or acknowledge us, but pitched his tent fairly close, although there was the whole of a huge field for him to choose from. Then he got out an old wind-up gramophone and played *Tiptoe Through The Tulips* while he set about building his fire and brewing tea. He played that same record over and over again until late in the evening. When we woke next morning he had gone – tent, gramophone and all. I can never hear that tune without thinking of him – whoever he was.

After I left school and joined Continental Express, I continued with my cycling, but I also decided to improve myself. Improve myself: that's a really old fashioned phrase, isn't it? But there is no other way to describe it. Like many another young fellow from a poor area, I thought my background and my accent would keep me back. Nowadays, when it is fashionable to have a local accent, such an idea might strike people as funny, but it was important, believe me, back in the late 1920s. If you wanted to 'get on', you had to improve yourself and so I set about doing this with vigour. I went to classes five evenings a week, learning German and French and what they called 'Public Speaking'. I do not know if Public Speaking is still taught at night schools, but as far as I was concerned it was a way of ironing out my broad Cockney and polishing off any other rough edges.

These days I suppose you would call it 'improving the image', but I knew nothing about image then. All I knew was that I wanted to escape from the East End and improving myself could provide the key. Although I have thought often about it, I do not think there was any particular reason why I chose to learn German although, as events were to prove, it was a fortuitous choice.

My friend Albert Goring, who had joined me in the lake at Loughton when we foraged for bullrushes and was my partner in other schoolboy schemes, encouraged me to go cycling and to attend these evening classes. He was a good influence on me, as well as a good companion. I always regarded him as an intellectual sort of chap, for he had the brains for study and did better than I did at school. He was top of the class and I was always near the bottom. After he left school he studied to become a librarian and spent all his life in the library service, apart from a spell in the RAF during the war. In Canning Town a librarian was looked on as someone special, and he was special to me.

So for five or six years my life settled into an uneventful pattern. I worked long hours in the City, attended my evening classes, and rode my bike at weekends and during the summer holidays. I scraped and saved all I could, but I was always hard up and there seemed to be no prospect at all of achieving my great ambition – to travel abroad.

I frequently rode my bike past Marble Arch and stared up at the flats on top of the Cumberland Hotel – this was where I would live one day, overlooking Hyde Park. In the meantime I observed the life of the people at the top by walking in through the front door of the Ritz in Piccadilly, admiring the opulent lobby, and wandering unnoticed out of the side door into Arlington Street. In fact, I still do just that if I want a taxi in that area when it is raining – but now the doorman knows my face.

Oh yes, travel abroad had become my goal, but surprisingly it was not a goal that Albert encouraged. He thought my ideas about travelling abroad were fanciful, but I determined that I would prove to him it was possible for us to get across the Channel and have a holiday, even though we were both hard up.

The first step in my plan was to tell my firm that I would take only one week of the fortnight's holiday due to me in 1933 if they would allow me to take an extra week the following year. In fact, I could only afford to go away for a week because I had spent too much of my money going out on Saturday nights with my mates. But when I explained that I wanted to take the extra week in order to go abroad on my bike they started off by being impressed but then pulled my leg unmercifully, because the idea of a kid like me taking a holiday 'on the Continong' just like the swells was absolutely ridiculous.

But they agreed that I could take just one week's holiday in 1933 and three weeks the following year, which, I had planned, would be the really important one. In a youth hostel I had met a young fellow cycling around the world. He came from Malaya (which might have been outer space for all I knew) and he lived on a small remittance sent to him by his family every month. A small plate fixed on his bike announced that he had left Malaya several months earlier, and the route he was taking around the world.

I was so intrigued by his adventurous journey that I devised a scheme by which I intended to do the same – cycle around the world sending a report of my adventures every month to 100 people who would pay me £1 per year for the privilege. I could then live on £1 per week and spend the other £1 per week on paper and postage to my subscribers.

Unhappily this scheme met with little success – in fact I failed to get a single subscriber! Nevertheless, the prospect of travelling abroad continued to excite me. What I did not know then was that 1934 would be just a few days old when something of monumental importance would happen.

I was to meet the girl who would become my wife.

As 1933 drew to a close, I began to get itchy feet, and the combination of restlessness and ambition drove me to improve my lot at work. I was already taking on all the odd jobs that were going in order to earn some extra money, but I felt I could be doing better. It was around this time that my father had to leave his grocery shop in Stephen's Road, because of the money he owed to the wholesalers, so maybe that insecurity was influencing my behaviour.

Whatever the reason, the boss of the Bucklersbury office finally called me into his room and asked me if I was prepared to move to Yorkshire and take up a post as assistant to the office manager there. By then my wage had been increased to thirty shillings from its original pound, and the Bradford job meant a rise of another £1 a week. What a tremendous prospect! I thought I would have money to burn, but the office manager pointed out that the extra £1 was to pay for my board and lodging. Not even the most enthusiastic of Canning Town cyclists would be able to travel each day between London and Bradford! It would mean leaving home for the first time in my life, but I was approaching 21 and old enough to make my way into the big world.

The first thing I did was go to the Fleet Street offices of the Bradford local newspaper – *The Telegraph and Argus* – and look through the adverts for rooms to rent. I wrote off to a Mrs Williams who was offering a room for 25 shillings a week all found, including washing. One of Mrs Williams's lodgers was a girl named Irene . . .

It was Irene who made the decision that I would stay at Mrs Williams's house, for there had been two letters inquiring about the room, one from me and the other from a policeman in Dewsbury who had been transferred to Bradford. Mrs Williams had asked Irene to decide and she had plumped for the London lad. To this day I do not know why she did, and I suspect she does not either, but that is the way we came to meet.

The date was January 15th, 1934. The day I travelled from London to Bradford. The first time I had ever been on a train – a real train, that is, not the London Underground.

I remember getting to King's Cross with my suitcase heavy and my hopes high. The firm had paid for my ticket and travelling expenses, so I decided to make the most of the experience. After getting used to the novelty of a railway carriage with a corridor, I ventured along it to the restaurant car. To have a meal on a train was, I thought, doing things in real style. I treated myself to a lunch and ordered a lager to go with it. Then I worried for an hour whether the firm would pay for the drink as well as the meal. I did not want to start off in Bradford on the wrong foot, so in the end I deducted the few pence that the lager had cost, and never claimed for it.

The journey was uneventful, and I made my way from the centre of Bradford to Mrs Williams's home. She greeted me in friendly style, showed me my room and told me about my fellow lodgers. There was one fellow she always referred to as 'Mr Smith-the-Chemist' as though that were his proper name. I expected to meet some weird professor, but he turned out to be a young chap of around my age who worked in Boots or Timothy Whites, or some such place. There was also a much older man who worked as a salesman for a sauce company – 'table sauces and associated condiments' was a phrase he often used. I never did discover the name of his firm, but he always smelled faintly of that brown, fruity sauce that was very popular at the time (and still is, for all I know).

And then there was Irene, who was described to me as 'a very nice young lady'. That evening, over high tea, I met them all. I was not very impressed by the other two, but I had my eye on the 'very nice young lady' from the start. Little did I know that she would become a financial genius and probably the highest paid businesswoman in Britain.

I discovered later that she came from near Bradford, but was living in digs because she had left home when she was 19. She had a stepfather who was unkind to her and, as she had taken a dislike to him, leaving home seemed a sensible solution. Like many others, her father had been killed in the First World War when she was only a year or two old. Her brother had also died in that war. He had lied about his age in order to join the army, and I remember Rene telling me how her mother had made a cake to send out to him for his 18th birthday. It came back just a few days after they had received the telegram telling them he had been killed. He had died a couple of days before his birthday. Anyway despite, or possibly because of, our very different character, immediately we met Rene and I were attracted to one another and have remained so through thick and thin ever since. I have always counted January 15th 1934 the luckiest day of my life.

The job in Bradford turned out to be something of a disaster because it was nothing like I had been led to expect. When they told me in London that I would be assistant to the office manager, I had expected to be working in an office as large at least as the one in Bucklersbury. That would have meant that I would have fellows working under me.

But, when I reported for work, I discovered I constituted the only staff there, apart from the office manager. I really was the jack of all trades, answering the telephone, sweeping the floor, making the tea and generally keeping the place tidy. I had to pack up the parcels – it was a freight forwarding office – put them into sacks and load the sacks onto the carts which came each night to take them to the railway station. I also had to load the lorries which we sometimes used for runs to London.

On top of that, I simply could not get on with the boss of this one-eyed establishment. We took an instant dislike to each other, and I did not help myself by telling him I was taking three weeks off that summer instead of two. He disputed this, knowing I was only entitled to a fortnight, and would not listen to my explanation. Well, when he checked with the London office and found out that I had been right, that simply made everything so much worse.

Looking back, I realise now that I must have been a bumptious little bastard, coming up from London and right away telling this chap more or less how to run the business. I believe he thought I was some sort of spy sent up to report on him, so the atmosphere was pretty poisonous.

And that is the way it was through the early months of that year. The only bright spot was Irene, back at my lodgings. And, of course, the prospect of my great adventure. As summer approached I prepared for my very first holiday abroad. A cycling trip to Germany.

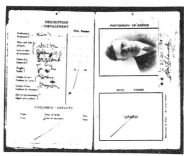

My first passport.

CHAPTER TWO

By Bike to Berlin

I HAVE NO words to describe the state of excitement I was in as I made my preparations for the trip to Germany. Perhaps you can imagine how I felt. Just thinking about going abroad was an adventure, and here I was, in the spring of 1934, actually making my plans. What might be most difficult to understand nowadays is that, at that time, I had never met anybody who had ever been across the Channel – except for my father and one or two others who had served in the First World War. Going abroad for a holiday was not for the likes of us down in Canning Town (or, in my case, up in Bradford).

But I was determined to make it and threw all my energies into the operation. I had to find out about getting a passport – and get one. I had to find out about the cheapest way to travel, for I was forced to keep within a very tight budget. I had to get maps of Germany and work out which route to take. I was convinced that, with all these preparations, we would make a go of it.

Oh yes, it was 'we' because I had persuaded my friend Albert Goring to join me. He was not too keen, as I recall, but he had sort of challenged me to do it and, as I had saved up that extra week's holiday, I was going to make sure he came with me.

I once read that the writer Jules Verne, when he was a young boy, planned a trip with his brother Paul. The two boys were going to sail their little boat down the Loire and right out into the Bay of Biscay. Jules worked out the whole journey in great detail, planning how far they could cover each day and where they would stop each night. The day before they were due to start, he decided not to go. The planning had been so exciting that he felt the trip itself would be an anti-climax. I know that happens to many people, especially when they spend a lot of time planning and choosing and looking forward to their holiday. For them, the anticipation is better than the reality.

But that is not my style now, and nor was it back in 1934. This trip was going to be done exactly according to plan. I briefed Albert in a letter and, on 29th of July, the great adventure began. I cadged a lift in a lorry from Bradford to London. That is not as haphazard as it might seem, because the freight office was right next door to the lorry yard and we used to send stuff down in the lorries almost every night. I had got to know the drivers, so getting a lift was easy. It was also free.

That journey brought me down overnight to the City and I went from there to my home in Hermit Road where I collected my bike. I also collected Albert, who was then working as a junior librarian in Canning Town. Together we rode off to Hay's Wharf, London Bridge, to go on board a Russian ship called the *Co-operazia*, which operated a service from the Thames to Leningrad via Hamburg. The return fare, London-Hamburg, was £3 each, including food. The bikes went for nothing.

And that was how we set off. The two days on the ship were uneventful, apart from our youthful excitement at being at sea, which was a brand new experience for both of us.

When we got to Hamburg, we stayed in a youth hostel which had been established on board an old sailing ship moored there. It was one of the old grain ships which had sailed to and from Australia more than a century previously. You were supposed to pay one mark per night – which was the equivalent of one shilling in those days, or five pence today. But if you were a student you could stay for 25 pfennigs, a quarter of the price. Naturally, we said we were students and in a way that was quite true. We were studying German and Geography at the University of Life!

The following day I completely staggered Albert by telling him we were going to travel on by air! I think he thought I was off my rocker, but an air trip fell neatly into my plans.

The German airline, Lufthansa, ran a daily service between Berlin, Hamburg and Cologne and, by studying the timetable, I had found a flight which left Hambrug just after six in the evening and arrived in Berlin at seven. I reckoned that it was a luxury we could afford because it would enable us to cover 255 kilometres in 50 minutes and save us a lot of pedalling. The single fare was 25 marks – 25 shillings.

Albert was not altogether sure about this and I must say I would not blame him, but I persuaded him of the advantages and pointed out that we would have something to tell our friends when we got home. Not only had we been abroad, but we had flown in an aeroplane. You would have to go a long way to top that around the East End!

We packed all our luggage into pannier bags which we slung on the backs of our bicycles. I knew the bikes could not go on the plane, so we rode them down to Hamburg Railway Station and sent them on to Berlin by rail. It was all done very efficiently and I had not a moment's doubt that the bikes would be waiting for us when we got to Berlin. Having got rid of the bikes we made our way to the airport and it was then I realised I had 'organised' us into a problem. We were overweight.

Nowadays, when air travel is more or less commonplace, people probably know all about weight restrictions on aeroplanes and the problems of excess baggage. Everybody preparing for a package holiday abroad knows what the luggage allowance is. But we had no idea that such restrictions existed. The main difficulty was that the plane used on the route – Lufthansa called it the *Blitzstrecke* or 'Lightning Route' – was a Heinkel He70 which had come into service with the airline the previous year, having broken several world speed records. It took only three or four passengers, according to weight, so it was essential that the little plane was carefully loaded and trimmed. Every passenger had to be carefully weighed, as did all the luggage.

When we turned up with our pannier bags, we were told that we could take only 10 kilos each as a free allowance and would have to pay heavily for the rest. I did not think this at all fair because, while the two other passengers were considerably bigger and heavier than us they were not expected to pay anything because they were overweight. But the ticket clerk explained that it was the weight of the baggage not the weight of the passengers that mattered. I had a quick consultation with Albert and we retrieved our bags, saying we would come back a little later.

We nipped smartly into the gents' lavatory and put on as much clothing as we could – three shirts under a couple of sweaters, our shorts worn under our trousers and two or three pairs of socks. We carried jackets over our arms and thus managed to reduce the weight of the bags to within the free allowance. Or perhaps the clerk, impressed by our enterprise, kindly decided that the bags were within the allowance!

We took off in the tiny Heinkel. It was very thrilling for a couple of kids, but I remember that our fellow passengers did not think much of us. One was a typical German businessman of the time, weighing about 20 stone and wearing an expensive dark suit and a homburg hat. The other was a woman, also on the plump side, but very good looking and smartly dressed. They looked down their noses at the two ragamuffins who had got on the plane with them, two youngsters whose clothes were bulging out in all directions. After a few minutes the plane began to shake about and the woman turned very pale as the captain handed out little bags to each of us.

She was the first to be sick and I whispered to Albert: 'That's one up to us'. Then the man was sick. I looked at Albert and Albert looked at me. That was two up to us. But not for long. By the time we got to Berlin, the score was even and four very wobbly passengers clambered out.

The bikes were waiting for us at the railway station, for the German system was extremely efficient. We collected them and set off for the next stage of the great adventure.

One of the reasons I had chosen to travel to Germany was to improve the little bit of German I had been learning at evening classes before I moved to Bradford. I knew a few words, but nowhere near enough to conduct a long conversation, and thought that by plunging in at the deep end, as it were, I would improve my knowledge. It did not work out that way. Just imagine how you would feel if you had never been abroad in your life and found yourself riding a bike on the wrong side of the road in a foreign land.

I knew where my carefully planned itinerary would take us, but arriving at Berlin airport was like arriving at Heathrow and trying to make your way to Bishops Stortford. We had to go right through the centre of Berlin, and at every street or two we would stop and ask the way. We used to ride two or three hundred yards in the direction that people indicated, then stop and ask again. We kangaroo-hopped our way across Berlin and set off on our tour of the Harz Mountains.

And so the trip went more or less according to plan. We stayed in youth hostels at the student rate, spent as little as possible on food, but tried living off the land. What that really meant was that we pinched a lot of apples!

It was on this journey that I first encountered Adolf Hitler – though not at first hand. We had heard his name back in England, of course, but I certainly knew very little about him. He had been elected to office in 1933, as I recall, but our 1934 visit coincided with another election campaign. I was not politically aware, so it meant nothing to me, but we both quickly discovered that the Germans took their politics and Herr Hitler very seriously indeed.

We thought it amusing that they all treated Hitler with such seriousness. When we entered a café, for instance, people would say 'Heil Hitler' instead of 'good morning' or 'good afternoon'. They said it with varying degrees of enthusiasm, and they also wrote it at the bottom of their letters. It was 'Heil Hitler' instead of 'yours sincerely'. There was certainly no getting away from the man or his influence on everyday life. He was determined to Germanise the vocabulary and replace foreign (mainly French) words with German substitutes. Public call boxes no longer had 'telephon' on them, but 'Fernsprecher', for example.

But the oddest experience we had was when we cycled into Halberstadt, a lovely old town with masses of half-timbered buildings and a thousand years of history.

It was the end of an exhausting day when we got to the youth hostel, so all we wanted was to get a meal and some rest. We pitched our packs on to the beds they had allocated us and went downstairs to find the kitchen and the dining room. There was a nice portly old dame there, so we asked for some meat and potatoes and ordered a couple of beers. After about ten minutes the radio on the dining room wall stopped playing music and announced that Herr Hitler was about to make a speech. We knew enough German to make that out and, like everyone else in the dining room, we sat and listened. And sat. And sat. Everybody else was listening with rapt attention, but nothing else was happening and, as neither beers nor our supper had arrived, I went out into the kitchen to find the old lady.

She was there, listening to her own little radio, and when I told her we were still waiting to eat she waved at me to be quiet and said she would serve us when Hitler had finished his speech. It was like having to sit still in church while the sermon was being preached.

We waited for a little while longer and in the end I told her to forget about the meal. We thought we would be better off going elsewhere. But we went all around that town and in café after café it was exactly the same. Everybody was listening to the Hitler speech. Nothing else was happening, no meals or drinks were being served. Everybody went hungry for an hour-and-a-half and it was well after ten by the time we got our meal.

I realised then – at the ripe old age of 21 – that there was something very peculiar about that country, or, rather, about the people, if they could all sit like that, mesmerised by a political speech. Of course, we could not understand all he was saying, except that we thought he must be a raving lunatic judging by the emotional pitch of his voice and all the screaming and thumping.

It seemed that President Hindenberg, who I had never heard of, had died, and this chap Hitler had become Chancellor, President and everything else rolled into one, and we began to realise that perhaps he was not just the comic character we had supposed.

By then our visit was coming to an end. We had, indeed, fallen a little bit behind the schedule I had planned and, by the time we reached Hanover, I realised that we were short of time if we were to catch the *Co-operazia* at Hamburg. So we had to take the train from Hanover instead of cycling, and that meant that we were literally down to our last few coppers. We had just about enough money to pay for the youth hostel, but nothing for food.

My solution to this problem lay in the fact that my employers, Continental Express, had an office in Hamburg. So I tidied myself up and went over to visit them, explaining that I was an employee from England on holiday in Germany and that I had had my wallet stolen. I asked them to lend me enough to see me through the day, and I would arrange to repay it as soon as I got back to the London office. It was a proper confidence trick, but they accepted the story without batting an eyelid. They lent me some money, so Albert and I were able to eat in Hamburg before boarding the ship back to London.

My plans had worked out, for the holiday fitted exactly into the three weeks I had been allowed. I hitched a night ride in another lorry back to Bradford and worked out my budget on the way north. The whole holiday had cost me £12. The biggest single expense had been the £3 return fare for the ship and the 25 shillings for the flight to Berlin from Hamburg. The rest had gone on youth hostel beds and meals.

The only thing I should add is that I cannot for the life of me remember whether I repaid the marks that were lent me by the Hamburg office! I like to think that I did.

After my great adventure abroad, it was impossible for me to settle back into the routine of the job in Bradford. Although Irene and I were getting along famously, I knew that I would have to get back down to London, so I took the plunge and wrote to our head office, telling them that I would have to leave Bradford because there were no opportunities for me. After a while they agreed to have me back in London and, although at the time I thought that it had been my letter that had done the trick, I suspect that the office manager in Bradford had also put his oar in, as he was anxious to be rid of me. I believe he thought I had been sent up to spy on him. But, whatever the reason, I ended up working back down in London in the accounts department. The drawback was that they cut my wages by £1 a week as I was no longer having to pay for lodgings. So there I was, back in London, earning just 30s. a week.

It was around this time – the end of 1934 – that my mother went into hospital. She had cancer of the throat, but when on my weekly visit I would ask how she was, she would always answer, 'Oh, about the same.' She never once complained about her condition, but I could see as the weeks passed that she was getting worse.

One day, when I arrived for my visit, the porter asked me to wait while he telephoned the ward. This was unusual, for he knew who I was and normally waved me in. But he made that telephone call then came and told me that my mother was dead. I had to return home and break the news to my father.

By now we were back in Hermit Road, the shop in Stephen's Road having gone bust. My father was managing to run his corner sweetshop and make a sort of living out of it but, like many other people, we were going through lean times as 1935 got into its stride.

A few months later I was working away in the office when somebody called me over to take a telephone call from 'a lady named Irene'. I thought at first she was calling from Bradford, but quickly realised she was down in London. 'On holiday?' I asked nervously. I was worried in case she had come down to London and wanted me to support her. When she told me she had left Bradford for good and wanted to make her way in London, I really thought she was chasing after me! 'It's no good coming down here to live,' I said, 'it's very expensive.' And then, in case she hadn't got the point, I added, 'And I've got no money.'

I could not have been more wrong. She already had a job as a temporary comptometer operator, working in the St. Paul's area. She was perfectly capable of managing by herself, she told me rather sharply, and she had only telephoned to let me know she was in London. There were definitely no strings attached.

I felt very foolish, I can tell you. And even more foolish a little later on when she telephoned again to say that, after doing one or two temporary jobs, she had got a permanent place with the Ford Motor Company at Dagenham. I nearly fell off my chair, because Fords was the place where everybody tried to land a job. Even I had tried, without success. Fords were always advertising for lathe operators, so I had applied without knowing what a lathe operator was. I thought I might be able to bluff it out, but fortunately for me – and for Fords – I did not even get an interview and to this day do not know what a lathe operator does.

But here was Irene, fresh down from Bradford, and she had got herself into the accounts department at Fords. I asked her how much they were paying, and she told me: £5 a week. Talk about the boot being on the other foot! I had thought that she wanted me to look after her and here she was earning more than three times as much as I was. I decided that this was a girl worth helping!

She had telephoned because she had to find accommodation near Dagenham; she had been staying in a YWCA in Baker Street but the travelling was too arduous and too expensive. By coincidence a chap sitting opposite me in the office had an aunt who took in lodgers at her house in Upminster, so that was where Irene went to live. In fact, that is why we live in Upminster today – but I shall get around to telling you about that a little later on. I do not want to rush ahead of myself because I was all set, back in 1935, to go off on another adventure abroad. Another trip to Germany.

It was to be the same sort of trip, very low budget and bikes all the way, and Albert Goring had agreed to join me again. I think he was really curious to find out what I would get up to next, or perhaps thought he had better come along to keep me out of trouble. As far as I was concerned, the trip began even better than the previous one because the boat journey cost us nothing. We rode down to Tilbury and asked around among the boats to find out if we could get a free ride to Antwerp. Eventually the skipper of a small boat said that he would take us over – it was as simple as that. As he was going to on the bridge, he said we could have his cabin, but the weather was so rough that sleep was out of the question. We were both violently ill and pretty scared.

Eventually I went up on deck, clinging on for dear life, and found the skipper at the wheel. He was standing like a rock, quite oblivious to the seas pounding over us and for the first time I felt safe.

I shall spare you all the details of the tour except to mention that we cycled from Antwerp to Brussels, where there was some big exhibition taking place, and then went all the way down to Munich and to Berchtesgaden. The town itself is very picturesque, but I must admit it was the connection with Adolf Hitler that drew us down there to see what we could of the 'Eagle's Nest' which had been constructed at Obersalzberg up above Berchtesgaden. He was in residence during our visit, and wherever we looked we saw men in very smart uniforms. I still had no real idea of what Hitler and his followers were like – although Albert took more interest in the political scene and had some strong ideas about them. I was to find out more a few days later when we crossed the border into Austria.

Because we had no documents for our bike (this time, by the way, we were riding a tandem that had been lent to us by a relative of Albert's), we had to get them from the local cycle club. The chap there did not know quite what we were after, but we assembled some impressive pieces of paper with stamps and signatures all over them and that satisfied the officials at the border. It was then I realised the importance of having an impressive piece of paper if you are trying to persuade an official to do something even a little bit out of the ordinary.

We were making for Seefeld, and had to start walking because it was three or four thousand feet higher, with a lot of enormous hills to cover. We walked for most of the day and arrived at about seven in the evening, staying in a little pension called the Karwendelhof.

Seefeld at this time was a tiny village with two or three pensions to which people used to go in the winter for skiing. It was not a summer resort, so it was virtually empty when we were there in August 50 years ago. It is difficult to believe that this is the same resort that today has more than 4,000 hotel beds and is one of the biggest holiday centres in Austria both for winter and summer. Yet in respect of its scenery, its mountains, its snow, its sun and its people, it has not changed at all.

The Karwendelhof is now a four star hotel, but it is still run by the same family as in those days so long ago. Elsa, whom I remember as a young girl living there with her parents, is married to the present owner Fritz Wilberger, and their son and daughter run the hotel. The most amazing character, however, is Elsa's mother, still active at 94 or 95 and still working – very lightly in the laundry. They tell me she comes in every day 'to do a little folding'. I absolutely fell for Seefeld and thought it would be a splendid place for a holiday.

But there was another side to Austria, in total contrast to the simple pleasures of Seefeld. And we saw this other, darker, side when we travelled on to Innsbruck and took a stroll along Maria Theresa Strasse. It is a lovely street with very smart shops, but to our amazement we saw soldiers standing outside many of these shops. They were not proper soldiers, or members of the elite SS, but the louts and hangers-on of the Nazi movement. There were a couple standing outside every Jewish owned shop, telling people that they could only enter these premises if they, too, were Jewish. The windows of these shops were whitewashed with 'Jewish–keep out' daubed all over them. Albert and I looked at this first in disbelief and then gradually realized it was not a sick joke. This was real. This was a portent of what was to come. These people were hateful.

Looking back with the benefit of experience and hindsight, it is easy to see that Hitler came to power because the Germans had nothing else to cling to and nobody else to turn to. The country had been smashed after the First World War, there was enormous inflation, great unemployment and pervading hopelessness. Along came Hitler and promised to put them back on their feet, restore pride in themselves and in their country. And he did. He gave them work and won their loyalty. In the words of the old cliché 'he made the trains run on time'. And he put them into

1934: *Russian ship* Co-operatzia *sailing from Tower Bridge with my bike and me bound for Berlin.*

1934: *Hitler's stormtroopers marching in Unter den Linden.*

1934: *Unemployed marching in the East India Dock Road on the 'Hunger March' in protest at the reduction of unemployment benefit from 17 shillings to 15 shillings per week.*

1934: *Hamburg Station, destroyed in the war.*

1934: *Hamburg airport. A Heinkel HE70 three or four seater of Lufthansa preparing for take-off to Berlin.*

1934: *The Reichstag, destroyed by fire the same year.*

uniforms – a nation that respects uniforms so much.

I recall getting a little involved with their 'Kraft durch Freude' movement during a later winter. I wanted to find out something more about this 'strength through joy' idea and went on one of their winter sports holidays. It was terrifying to see these youngsters of 18 to 20, travelling on special trains in order to go on holiday together, worshipping the state and demonstrating their loyalty to the Führer. They were being bred to it and the sight of them made me realise that awful trouble lay ahead.

But that came later. In the meantime we were heading home from Austria, cycling back through Switzerland, all the way along Lake Constance, and through Basle back into Germany. We settled into a regular pattern of progress, Albert and I, spending hours walking up hills and then freewheeling down with our feet off the pedals. The roads were pretty rough, so it was no surprise when we broke the forks of the tandem. We tried to have them repaired in Freiburg, but without success, so we put the bike on the train (a familiar procedure by now) and spent three days walking through the Black Forest – in the rain. Then it was back to Antwerp to catch the boat for London. Another German adventure was over.

But not quite. For on this trip I discovered something that was to change my life completely. And all because I thought I had stumbled upon a way of getting free holidays.

I can pin it down to a particular place – not Seefeld, which I really liked and which was one of the first places I featured in my organised holidays. It was the tiny village of Schwangau, which had no claim to fame but which did have a youth hostel where we stayed. It also had a couple of pensions, one of which was the local pub where some English people were staying on holiday. When I saw them, I realised that people from England were paying money to go to Schwangau, and it did not take me long to find out that they were there with a firm called the Workers' Travel Association. The WTA had started that year as an offspring of the trades union movement, and the fact that these ordinary working people were able to go abroad for a holiday marked the beginning of what we now know as a popular 'package tour'.

The group numbered 50 and each had paid about £10 for the fortnight's holiday. Having had considerable experience in working out the budgets for our own holidays (!), I had the idea that I could organise the same holiday, but cheaper than the WTA. So I took myself across the road to the other pension, the Weinbauer, which was more of a wine bar than a pub and seemed to me to be definitely superior. I asked the owner what his rates were and he told me – six marks per day for full pension. That did not seem very much, even in those days. At that time there were 20 marks to £1, so that meant just six shillings a day for a room and three meals.

On my return to London I took the first opportunity of going down to Victoria Station and asking about the fares to Schwangau. The return fare was a little under £5 but, if I organised a party of 15, I would get the fares for 25 per cent less – and one free place. And that was what interested me at once – the free ticket and the possibility of free holidays for the rest of my life!

Yes, believe it or not, I had no thought of making any money from organising holidays. I thought only about the free place that I could have if I got a party together. So I worked it all out and prepared a little leaflet which I ran off on a duplicating machine, offering two weeks for ten guineas. I also put an advertisement in the *Daily Telegraph* and *The Times*: 'Young man going to Bavaria willing to take paying guests', or words to that effect. 'Ten guineas, two weeks.'

In the summer of 1936 five people responded, all of them elderly and all interested in going into the mountains to pick flowers. I remember one of them vividly because he was a very keen botanist who took a lot of persuading. He phoned me up a dozen times and asked if there was edelweiss in the area. I told him there was plenty of it, but prayed that he would not prolong the conversation because I had no idea what edelweiss was. What it all amounts to, I suppose, is that I told him and all the others exactly what they wanted to hear. I said yes to everything, promising that it would be exactly the way they wanted it to be. You could not tell such stories these days, for the Fair Trading people would be on you like a ton of bricks. But back then it was all fair game.

That first trip taught me a vital and very basic lesson: the price of failure. It was a failure for two reasons. First because I wanted 15 people and got only five. That meant that I had to pay full fares because I could not take advantage of the party rate. And I had to pay for myself, too. So did Albert.

It is a lesson that is as true today as it was all those years ago, and one that any tour operator ignores at his peril. You have to get the load factor right. It does not matter how big a business is, the bottom line is the load factor. And five out of fifteen simply was not good enough. The second lesson was the sensitivity of the tour operator's business to factors beyond his control – war, the threat of war, the strength of the pound, even the weather. This time, and not for the last time, it was Hitler. Against all the conditions of the Treaty of Versailles, the German army marched into the Rhineland and no one lifted a finger in protest. But it received plenty of adverse publicity, which is why I only had five bookings instead of the hoped-for fifteen.

Anyway, we took our little group to Schwangau on the train, put them up at the six shillings a day pension and tried to keep them amused. Our plan was to get them to walk around the village, do a little shopping and generally take it easy on one day, promising that the next day we would take them on an excursion.

Of course, while they were relaxing, Albert and I would dash off on the tandem to research the excursion, buy a pamphlet and learn all about the place. The next day we would take them all out in a taxi and tell them what they were going to see. They thought I was a very knowledgeable fellow, but it was all knowledge cribbed from the pamphlets. It was on this trip that I learned how I could make money without actually working for it. And I learned that from a taxi driver.

At the end of one excursion, having acted as a guide on a taxi tour, I got my people back to the pension and, as I was ushering them inside, was approached by a chap who asked if I would consider using his taxi for the trips in future. He spoke in German, of course, but by then my knowledge of the language was improving, so I was able to conduct a conversation with him. He asked me if I was a guide, and when I told him I was not only a guide but also the tour leader (which sounded very impressive, especially in German) he said he would pay me a ten per cent commission if I used his vehicle.

I had never heard about commission, but very quickly grasped the idea. 'But if you pay me ten per cent, does that mean you will charge my customers more than other taxis?' I asked. He assured me that his price was exactly the same as other drivers would charge and that the commission would come out of his profit not their pockets. Until this time I had worked long hours at tedious tasks to earn small wages. Suddenly with a flash of inspiration, I realised I could earn more money without working, and the magic word was commission. Into the bargain, I would realise my ambition to travel. I would be a travel agent. So that is how I learned about commission and, although I had a certain struggle with my conscience to begin with, I realised that this was the way people did business. Well, most people. I myself pay no commission on my holiday sales because I do not use travel agents – but we will come to all that later on.

That single trip in 1936 was the full extent of my tour operating activities and I certainly made no money out of it. However, as I had done it during my normal holiday from work, I still had my proper job to keep me going. But then my salary was £2 a week, which was just as well because it seemed that taking people on holiday was not going to be a paying proposition.

But, you know, the more I thought about it the more I felt I could make a go of it . . .

Finally, after wondering and worrying and trying to weigh up all the different angles, I decided to take the plunge. I was 23 years old and I was going to become a Travel Agent and Holiday Tour Organiser. It sounded very impressive when I told the clerks in the office, but I knew that they all though I was crazy to consider giving up a steady job for nothing but a dream. Those 'free holidays' could cost me everything I had. But I had to give it a try.

CHAPTER THREE

Taking the Plunge

STANDING in a corner of the assembly room at the Grove School, Stratford, E.15, I watched the crowd milling about and listened to the band that was playing for the dances. But I watched and listened with only half my attention. A lot of weightier things were giving me cause for concern that February evening. Every now and then somebody would come up and grab my shoulder or pump at my hand, introducing himself and trying to recall our times together at the Grove School. The faces and the names were familiar, but as I was really in no mood for reminiscing, the conversations did not last long. I suppose they thought me rude and perhaps they were right, for I just was not in the right frame of mind to enjoy a school reunion dance.

I had firmly made up my mind to chuck in my job and become a tour operator – a 'holiday-party organiser' was the generally accepted term in those days – and the realisation of what I had done was sinking home. The euphoria of the autumn had dribbled away through the gloomy winter, and I was glad that I had decided to hang on to my job in the City until the last possible moment. That £2 a week salary was all I had to see me through. My father thought that, through a friend on the West Ham Council, I might be able to get a job as a tram conductor, 'a regular job, with a pension at 65'.

I was in that frame of mind – and I am sure you know what I mean – when my common sense was telling me to hang back and forget the whole stupid idea, while my pride was urging me to throw caution to the winds and press ahead. If I ignored my pride and took the sensible course, nobody would know. Nobody but me. And that is what made it worse. I would know that I had turned away from the challenge, and I would have to live with that knowledge.

In case you are thinking that I was making heavy weather of all this, just remember what the prospects were for an out-of-work clerk in 1937. And bear in mind that I was 23 years old – that age when young men think they can conquer the world and know that if they do not make a move in that battle they will be saddled with whatever the world deals out to them – the boring job, the family responsibilities, the mortgage hanging round their necks. I *was* going to conquer the world, in my own fashion. But, oh, what a struggle it was proving to be!

A hand fell on my shoulder and I heard someone say: 'Chandler, isn't it?' I turned, expecting to find another contemporary waiting to introduce a wife or girlfriend and tell me about his job or ask me if I knew what had happened to old so-and-so. To my surprise, it was the headmaster himself, E. H. Madden, BA, BSc, 'Old Maddy' to his pupils, but not to his face.

Straight away I thought of all the scrapes I had got into during my time at the school and all the times I had been on the receiving end of his discipline. I had always thought of him as a stern man and even now, on a social occasion with his wife at his side, he still had that ability to turn me into a nervous schoolboy again. I stuttered out some kind of greeting, but he just nodded it away and asked what I was doing these days. I think he had heard about my joining Continental Express, and probably expected me to tell him about my shining prospects in the world of commerce. But I found myself telling him about my plans to become a holiday party organiser, and of my enthusiasm for Bavaria and Schwangau, the resort I had chosen to 'promote' as a holiday entrepreneur.

To my surprise he paid close attention, nodding enthusiastically and complimenting me on my enterprise. I suddenly had a brainwave. 'Do you think I could get a copy of the membership list?' I asked. 'I mean, the members of the Old School Association. I could write and tell them about my holidays. Perhaps they'd support . . .'

He stopped me in full flow. 'I've a much better plan, Chandler,' he said, with all that old headmasterly authority. 'We'll tell them about it right now.'

And before I knew what was happening, he steered me through the dancers towards the little stage, clambered up beside the band and pulled me up as well. The music faltered away as he held up his hand for silence. Then he made a short speech, introducing me as 'one of our former students who has had a very advanced idea', then, after a handful of sentences, pulled me forward to face the crowd.

I tried, vainly, to remember all the things they had taught me at the public speaking classes at the Evening Institute. It was no good. I could not make a 'proper' speech, not to that crowd of school friends and acquaintances. So I told them, as simply as possible, of my plan to sell holidays abroad. The main problem was that most of them believed holidays abroad were not for the likes of us. You had to be rich or 'a toff' to be able to afford to go across the Channel – to be the kind of people that got their photos in the papers as they relaxed on somebody's yacht along the French Riviera, or travelled to America on the big liners. Members of the Grove School Association did not see themselves falling naturally into that category.

But I tried to explain that they could afford a holiday abroad, and I told them I would send them all details of my wonderful holidays in Bavaria. I painted a glowing picture of Schwangau before scrambling off the stage in a state of great confusion.

A few people came up to me asking for more details and telling me to make sure I sent them my leaflet. I thought they were simply being polite. I really did not know how the evening would turn out, but the headmaster had no doubts.

'Are you able to accept bookings this evening?' he asked. Then, seeing the puzzled look on my face, added, 'what I mean is, Mrs Madden and I have decided to go to Bavaria this summer, and we want to reserve our places now. We want to be your customers.'

I left the school feeling ten feet tall. All my doubts – well, most of them – had been resolved. I had arranged to collect the membership list of names and addresses from the Association secretary. Before a week was out, they would all get letters and leaflets from me.

Without realising it, I had stumbled on one of the most important factors behind a successful holiday tour operating business: a good mailing list. As the days and weeks passed, so the bookings began to come in. I do not think I had to place any newspaper advertisements in 1937, or at any rate, if I did, they made very little difference. The leaflet and the mailing list proved to be the basis for a good season.

I continued to work at Continental Express right up until the weekend of my first departure, in early June I think it was. I handed in my notice, all very proper, and at the end of the last working day I received the handshakes and the good wishes of the other clerks – and even of the Chief Accountant. I left Bucklersbury with very mixed feelings. There was apprehension of course, for I had absolutely no way of knowing if I had done the right thing. There was relief, because I never felt that I could fit into the day-to-day life of a City office. And, I suspect, there was some relief on their part, too. They were free, at last, of the East End misfit with ideas above his station.

Next day I accompanied my first little group to Schwangau taking them by train and cross-Channel ferry, just as Albert and I had done the previous year. At the end of the two week holiday I returned to Hermit Road to do all the clerical work for a week, before going off with another group to repeat the whole process.

Schwangau was just a small village, but two miles away was Fussen which proved to be a popular resort, and the holiday gave excellent value for money, or so I thought. For ten guineas my 'clients' were provided with return railway travel (third class) between London and Augsburg, by way of Dover, Ostend and Cologne. The ferry crossing was also included in the price, as was the coach transfer between Augsburg and the resort hotel. They also had lunch at Augsburg on the outward journey and full board accommodation at the hotel I had chosen in Schwangau – the Hotel Weinbauer. My leaflet held out the delights of the nearby tennis courts and promised plenty of opportunities for dancing in the local cafés. As for Fussen itself, the leaflet explained: 'situated on the ertswhile Austro-German frontier, it possesses all the attributes that one usually associates with a holiday resort – fine shops and cafés, magnificent surroundings, friendly mountain people, a jolly night life – and at the same time is far enough removed from the usual tourist routes to retain in a large measure its unspoiled natural charm'. Who could resist such a description?

That year I worked harder than I had ever worked in my life, accompanying the groups to Schwangau and Fussen and having little time in between to do much more than sort out the bookings, drum up new business, and answer letters. But that first year was a great success and, at the end of the holiday season, I had taken five or six parties abroad and had never had less than 20 people each time. That meant I could take advantage of the group discount on train fares and the free places, so the season was profitable. As the summer of 1937 came to its end I found myself with more money than I had ever had in my life. About £100.

I could see no barrier to my success. All I had to do was repeat the experience in 1938, perhaps on a larger scale. I laid my plans. The first thing was to replace the little leaflet with a more ambitious brochure, Albert Goring had helped me with the leaflet, so I turned to him for help in writing up the brochure – the prospectus, he called it. I had decided to change my centre from Schwangau to the more sophisticated resort of Fussen on the Austro-German frontier. Albert produced a glowing description of Fussen and another of a second destination I had decided to feature in 1938 – Berchtesgaden, which I had visited in 1935, and where Herr Hitler had built his retreat, the 'Eagle's Nest'.

And I decided to introduce another improvement at a supplement. The previous year we quoted only one price, 10 guineas, which covered third class travel and as I explained in my travel notes 'as the journey from London to Switzerland takes 24 hours and trains in Europe in third class have wooden seats you are advised to bring with you a rubber cushion'. The older generation found this a bit hard, so I decided to offer second-class travel at a supplement of two pounds ten shillings. This meant that my free ticket could be second class also, although I always found it more comfortable to travel stretched out in the luggage rack in the roof of the carriage so long as I could evade detection by the train conductor.

I sent out the brochure in January to all the people on my mailing list and, remembering the success of my evening at the Grove School, decided to try the same trick elsewhere.

This was the Russell School, which I had also attended. I went along to the annual dance, made a speech appealing to their loyalty to a fellow ex-pupil, and got more names and addresses for my mailing list. I repeated the process at a place called the Fifty-Fifty Club and ended up with more than 3,000 names on my list.

I felt that nothing could go wrong, as the bookings began to flow in.

But something did go wrong. In the spring of 1938 German troops marched across the border into Austria. Herr Hitler had decided on an *Anschluss* – a connection – so Austria was annexed on March 12th.

The failed art student who had left Vienna for Munich just about 25 years previously had come back with a vengeance. For the second time in my life – but not the last, as events were to prove – I learned how international politics can play havoc with the holiday business. Now please do not misunderstand me, for I know as well as you do what terrible consequences were to flow from those events of 1938. But at the time those consequences were unknown to me, and all I could think of was that my holiday tours were going to be ruined by the German action.

Because both my resorts were on the Austro-German border, they got massive publicity that spring, but it was the kind of publicity I could have done without – pictures of marching soldiers in all the newspapers, and the names of Berchtesgaden and Fussen in the headlines. The customers began to cancel their bookings, but I hoped that I could still manage if I withdrew the Berchtesgaden holidays and concentrated everything on Fussen.

I took my little groups away, as I had in the previous year, but they were indeed little groups with never more than half a dozen people at any time. That meant no discounted fares and no free places, so I lost most of the money I had made in 1937. It taught me another valuable lesson – that good times and lean times are never far apart in the holiday business and that anything can happen to ruin the best laid plans. It is an experience I have had many times since 1938, as you will learn.

Anyway, I managed to struggle along until the end of the summer season and withdrew to lick my financial wounds. I was almost literally skint and all I wanted to do was keep body and soul together during the winter, so I could try again the next year. I was not concerned about war, mind you, in spite of all the stories and speeches reported in the papers. I realised that Austria and Germany might be finished as holiday destinations, but during my last trip I had travelled to Sarnen in Switzerland and believed that this little resort in the Bernese Oberland would set me back on my feet. In the meantime there was the small problem of making ends meet.

I had no work and the shop was faring badly, so my father was unable to help. The only member of the family working was my brother Bill. Olive and Arthur were still at school. There was no way in which Bill could support us all, so I set out to make money whichever way I could. I started off by going to work as a debt collector for the owner of a local radio shop (which is still going strong, as a matter of fact). I had treated myself to a motor bike on the profits of 1937 and managed to hang on to it in spite of my subsequent problems. So I used it to go around the houses of this chap's customers.

They had bought radios on the never-never, promising to pay off the money at the rate of a shilling a week. My job was to do the rounds of the houses on pay day and screw the shillings out of the customers. I remember that the weather was really terrible and depressing, as if the job itself had not been depressing enough. I was not very good at getting the money because, if people did not pay, the ultimate threat was that I would take the radio set back – and frankly they did not mind parting with the sets. They had had them for a few months and would probably work the same deal on some other shop.

I had to gather them up, festoon them around the motor bike and make my way back to the shop with them at the end of the day. This arrangement suited me, because it meant that I need not keep going back to the houses to get the shillings. But it certainly did not suit the boss. Instead of an income, he was getting a lot of battered and very second-hand radio sets.

'Now you look here,' he told me in the end, in a fit of exasperation, 'I'm not going to fill up this shop with a lot of second-hand radios. My business is selling new ones and your job is collecting the money. If you can't get the money, then you'd better pack in the job.' So that is what I did.

That was the end of that job, but in many ways it paralleled my father's experience earlier when he had gone bust in his little corner shop. I did not have the heart to screw money out of people who could not afford to pay just as he had not had the heart to refuse credit to families who could not otherwise afford food. I know that in business you are supposed to have firm rules and a sensible head on your shoulders, but how can you apply those rules when you know the financial circumstances of the customers who are also your neighbours? I am not that kind of person. I am not ruthless like some of these tycoons you read about. I suppose I might have a different attitude if I was part of some big company, but when you run your own business you have to live with your own decisions. I have never been able to sack anybody, for instance. I would be hopeless at that.

Anyway, let us not digress again. I was telling you about the odd jobs I took on to keep going through that rotten winter. One of them was working for the Post Office, and that was really money for old rope. I applied to be a sorter, but was not considered good enough for that and so was given a job as a porter at a shilling an hour. For three weeks I did night duty, but it was a real con trick, because I only did one hour's work and slept through the rest of the shift. I am told it is still just the same and anybody looking for a soft job should work nights for the Post Office; for a few weeks up to Christmas!

During the day, of course, I spent my time looking for another and better paid job, or even one I could do in addition to the night duty. However, one morning my father came into my room just as I was about to get up and told me there was a businessman downstairs waiting to see me. It sounded pretty impressive and I was certainly impressed when I went downstairs and saw this fellow.

He looked exactly right for the part and had all the right kind of talk, which should have warned me from the start that he was something of a confidence trickster.

His story was that he manufactured pin tables – simple slot machines operated by the insertion of a penny coin and nothing like the sophisticated gaming machines available nowadays. These were installed in several sleazy East End cafés frequented mostly by the unemployed to pass the time away, I suppose. In addition to making and supplying them, he also drew profits from them, in a loose kind of partnership with the café proprietors. He had come to me because he had heard I was a shrewd businessman and, as he was about to go to Australia, he wanted to sell his business to me.

For £20 I could take his place and draw the profits from the slot machines.

Well, £20 was every penny I had in the world, but he talked me into it and next morning I set out to do the rounds of my new gambling empire, calling on the cafés and introducing myself as the new owner of the machines. They were there, all right. All in dirty little cafés and all in need of some repair or other. I got a few coppers out of some of them and kept hoping it would get better. But it never did.

It was always the same story. The café owners would tell me that no sooner had I left the previous week than the machine had broken down and there was no money in it. I would fix the break and go away knowing there would be nothing there the next week either. The café owners knew I would be coming around on the Friday afternoon, so on the Friday morning they would simply break open the machines and take all the money out. I knew they were doing this. And they knew I knew. But what could I do? I was little Harry Chandler and these were big and tough East Enders. If I tried to outsmart them and pay a surprise visit during the week, they would stand over me waiting for their share of the money, and the menace was not worth the few pence involved. Things might have been different if I had had a 'minder'.

I kept it up for a while, but could see no way around the problem of their dishonesty, so in the end I took all the machines away and got rid of them for scrap.

But I was easy to fool in those days and, true enough, I got caught more than once again before the winter was out. I saw an advertisement in the paper: 'Interesting business opportunity for young man with £10 to invest', and went along to the address given. It was a sweet shop in Lewisham run by a woman whose husband worked in the Passport Office. He had, apparently, realised that holidays were a growing thing and thought she should start up a business to cash in on this new popularity. Or so her story went.

She told me she had a travel agency office in Shaftesbury Avenue and wanted a little more capital. She talked me into giving her the money – I think it might have been £20 rather than the £10 in the advertisement –

on the promise of a weekly wage and a share of the profits as the business built up. I could start on Monday morning at 9 am in the office. So I went along to Shaftesbury Avenue and, sure enough, there was this woman in her office, with its leaflets and travel posters, a couple of desks, a telephone and a typewriter. After settling me in, she went away and left me to it.

I spent two weeks there and not a single person came near the place, not even the woman. The telephone never rang and the post was nothing more than leaflets and circulars. Then, one Friday afternoon, a fellow came in and produced an unpaid bill for printing he had done something like six months previously.

'I'm just the clerk here, sir,' I said. 'I don't know anything about this, but I'll speak to Mrs Blank over the weekend and make sure the money is here for you on Monday morning.' I laid it on a bit thick, but convinced him that I was just a small time employee (which I was, really) and had neither the authority to pay him nor the money to do so. He stamped out, promising to be on the doorstep at nine o'clock on Monday morning and threatening all sorts of reprisals if the money was not forthcoming.

I watched him down the Avenue until he was out of sight, then I emptied my desk drawers, picked up the typewriter and left the office, locking the front door. Of course, I never went back. I did not even bother going over to Lewisham to try to get my money back from the woman, but decided to chalk the whole thing up to experience yet again. I kept that typewriter for some years, although the 'e' was missing, and sold it after the war.

I still had not learned my lesson and a little later I invested £10 with a woman who told me she was a professional gambler at Monte Carlo. If I would finance her for an experimental day at the casino in Ostend she would let me have a half share in her foolproof gambling system at roulette. I fell for the story once again, but of course I lost my money. In fact everything I have ever tried outside the travel trade has ended up in the same way: I always lost money.

Somehow or other, picking up odd jobs here and there, I survived the winter and prepared to launch my travel business once again in 1939. At that time I had no business name other than my own, but my letter heading was fairly impressive, or so I thought. It had the device of a globe with my initals 'HWC' within it, surmounted by the motto 'Holidays With Character' (HWC, get it?). It announced to the world that I was an organiser and host for British and continental holiday parties as well as an agent for the leading tourist agencies and all British holiday camps. My telephone number (actually, it was our telephone number at the shop in Hermit Road) was Albert Dock 1554, but I abbreviated the Albert Dock to ALB, hoping people would think that it was short for Albemarle, which gave a much better impression: West End rather than East End.

In February, 1939 I sent out my brochure to the 3,000 or so people on my mailing list. Even today, it is easy to spot the hand of Albert Goring in the wording of the accompanying letter: 'That period of the year during which holiday-party organisers hibernate more or less comfortably in their winter quarters is now past, and once more we bring out our dusty wares and decide what can be done to refurbish them for the coming season. For the third year I have pleasure in bringing my summer programme to your notice'.

Good old Albert. That 'more or less comfortably' was a touch of irony I did not appreciate at the time. In view of what 1939 was to have in store, the next paragraph contains ironies that neither of us appreciated. 'I suppose it is common knowledge that 1938 was rather a poor year for all Continental travel. This may have been due in part to the feeling that English visitors, particularly visitors to Germany, were not as welcome as in previous years. Those who came with me to Fussen last year, however, know how false this impression was; our reception was as cordial as ever before, and many agreed that the holidays were even happier than those of 1937. So much for last year. Let us now look forward to the summer holidays of 1939.'

The brochure offered information about a cycling tour of Denmark and holidays to the South of France, as well as to hotels in the Kent seaside resorts and various holiday camps in Britain, as I was acting as agent for those. But my very own holidays were a couple of trips to Fussen (though I did not hold out much hope for them) and half a dozen trips to Sarnen in Switzerland.

Sarnen is a small medieval town on the edge of a lake some 20 miles south of Lucerne. I had arranged to use the Hotel Waldeim, about two miles from the centre of the town itself. To quote again from my 1939 brochure: 'Picture if you can a chalet deep set in trees with smooth lawns and flower beds sloping gently down towards the crystal clear waters of Lake Sarnen; around for a thousand square miles stretches the mighty expanse of snow-covered peaks which form the Pennine Alps and the Bernese Oberland. This will give you some idea of the fine situation of the Hotel Waldheim on Lake Sarnen'.

I was offering 15-day holidays for ten guineas, on the same basis of two weeks out, and a week home for me to catch up on the paperwork. I was getting good bookings and reckoned to make ten shillings profit from each customer, having decided that ten guineas was the proper price to charge. But having met that enterprising taxi driver in Germany, I also realised I could make more profit in the form of commission out of the excursions (and that is still the situation to this day in respect of motor coach tours). So the brochure made a point of emphasising the various excursions that could be taken.

At the start of the holiday season I went to Sarnen and met the man who ran the local post coaches, Herr Dillier. These were horse-drawn as there were no motor coaches in the area at that time. I made arrangements for him to provide the transport for all my excursions, although he had no vehicle big enough to do the job. He said that if I could guarantee the business, he would buy a 30-seater motor coach on the strength of it. I gave him my guarantee, he went out and bought the coach. That same coach was still in operation until a few years ago and to this day stands in the garage of the Dillier Bus Company, now a substantial concern still in the ownership of the Dillier family with Hans Dillier as its managing director, the grandson of Joseph Dillier with whom I started business 50 years ago.

I started up a busy programme for my customers. The most popular and breathtaking excursion from Lucerne was the Three Passes Tour – over the Furka, the Grimsel and the Axenstrasse to the Rhone Glacier – which passed through magnificent scenery but which was also very expensive. It cost something like 35 francs then, but I learned that Herr Dillier could do it for about a quarter of that price. I knew that, if I could fill his coach every fortnight, on that alone I could make a handsome profit.

It was essential to have excursions on this holiday because the hotel was isolated and, if the weather was bad, guests had nothing to do. They quickly got tired of boating and swimming so my plan was to offer five or six excursions, more or less on the basis of one every other day. I used to tell people the evening beforehand what the excursion was to be and how much it would cost, but I quickly learned that this was not a good way of doing business. If the guests had gone shopping in Sarnen or had spent their money in the hotel bar, they would not have enough to buy an excursion. Or if they had had a late night and did not fancy an early morning start, they would back out. The same applied if it was raining.

That is only human nature, after all. But it was not good for business.

So I developed a scheme which I have stuck to, with very little variation, right up until the present day. This is to have an excursion 'Master Ticket' which is sold with the holiday in advance. Once a customer has bought this, he does not get his money back, so he comes on the excursions, rain or shine. It is better for him, too, because he has pleasant memories of the things he has seen on the trips, which he would have missed if he spent his time and money in the hotel bar!

The Hotel Waldheim was a simple picturesque wooden chalet in typical Swiss style, with about 20 bedrooms (some of them I proudly announced even had hot and cold running water). It was owned by Mr and Mrs Dansky, a White Russian emigré married to a Swiss, with two baby daughters. What impressed me most, however, was the hotel's magnificent position on the edge of the lake with the mountains as the backdrop of the other side of the lake, looking like a stage setting for White Horse Inn.

I had one small problem with what are euphemistically called in the travel trade the 'facilities'. The Waldheim boasted few wc's and this caused a problem when we left early in the morning on excursions. There was only one bathroom in the hotel, which all the guests had to share with the owners' family. When asked about getting a bath I said they should apply in writing giving a few days notice and it would cost 1 franc, or alternatively they could take a bar of soap into the lake. 50 years later the Waldheim still features in our brochure, owned and managed by one of the 'baby daughters' now married to Paul Townend, who first went there as our rep. many years ago, still in the same magnificent scenery, but, I hasten to add, with somewhat improved 'facilities'.

And so the summer of 1939 got under way. I was getting good bookings for my tours to Sarnen and after a couple of months the prospects were bright. I knew that the international situation was still volatile but, like most people, hoped that the politicians would be able to talk us through the various crises that erupted. As far as my personal fortunes were concerned, it looked as though H. W. Chandler, the 'Holidays With Character' man, had bounced back from a bad patch and was once again on the road to success. My holidays to Switzerland were doing really well and my thoughts were turning to the future.

What I did not know – what nobody knew – was that Herr Hitler, the man whose speech in 1934 had kept me from my dinner, was going to upset my plans once more.

Of the 300 people I had booked in that summer, a group of 40 was due to leave London at the end of August. On August 26th, 1939 to be precise.

CHAPTER FOUR

Caught Offside

A S I WALKED across the concourse of Victoria Station it seemed to me that there were more uniforms about than usual, even allowing for the fact that it was a Saturday morning when many servicemen were probably on weekend leave. The station was busy, but I had known it to be busier on those other Saturdays when I had waited there to meet my holiday groups. It was a tradition to meet 'under the clock', everybody did, so I tried to get there early in order to make my presence known to my customers. On that Saturday, August 26th, 1939, I could see no other holiday company representative except a couple of chaps from Cooks, whose uniforms did not seem at all out of place that day. They were standing near a large notice on an easel, informing Cooks customers that all holiday tour departures for the Continent had been cancelled 'in view of the international situation'. There were other similar notices in the concourse from the Polytechnic Touring Association and from WTA the Workers' Travel Association.

That international situation did seem to have taken a turn for the worse. Back in March, Mr Chamberlain had warned Germany against its policy of domination by force, after it had annexed Bohemia and Moravia and taken Slovakia 'into protection'. Herr Hitler had paid no attention and started a hate campaign against Poland. To me, the summer had flashed by in a whirl of activity. I was going backwards and forwards with my holiday groups to Switzerland while the politicians were making speeches and signing pacts right, left and centre. The previous month, Mr Chamberlain had confirmed our pledge of assistance to Poland but, all through that August, the German press had increased its anti-Polish campaign and there had been demonstrations in Danzig.

That very week had seen the screw tightening. On the Wednesday the Germans had signed a non-aggression pact with the USSR and begun making final preparations for an invasion of Poland. On the Friday an Anglo-Polish treaty had been signed in London.

So I had a lot on my mind, as I waited under the clock for my group to assemble. Having had my little business ruined in 1936 by the occupation of the Rhineland and again in 1938 by Herr Hitler's *Anschluss* with Austria, I was in no mood to let him repeat the process now.

Gradually the group assembled, and I was glad to see that just about all the 40 or so had turned up. I was not happy, though, when they began to tell me their worries and their doubts about travelling abroad at a time of such grave crisis. I invited them all into the station bar for a drink, hoping to talk them round, arguing that the other tour companies were over-reacting. Everybody knew that the British Foreign Office closed down for the weekend, and this fact was exploited by Herr Hitler. He knew that he could make a big speech or drop some thunderbolt on the world's press on a Friday evening and get no response from Britain until Monday morning. That is just what he had done the previous evening, with a speech about Germany's claims to Poland. 'It will all have blown over by Monday morning,' I said. 'Why don't we go home and meet again here on Monday. You'll see everything differently then, mark my words.'

Of course things did not blow over, but I returned to Victoria on the Monday morning, nursing the last remnants of my optimism. About a dozen of my customers were there, most of whom had only come to tell me that they were cancelling the holiday. I was left with five, of whom I remember in particular a chap who lived in London, an Australian and a middle-aged woman who had a leg iron. I was not too keen on taking her, because I realised there might be danger for us all. The men were a different proposition as they were now regarding the whole thing as an adventure. The woman was not to be dissuaded, however. 'I've paid you my ten guineas,' she declared. 'If you go, then I'm coming with you and that's the end of it. Well, what do you say?'

What could I say? We gathered up our suitcases and got on the train for Dover. The ferry would take us to Ostend and another train carry us to Strasbourg, Basle and Lucerne. It was a strange experience for me to be able to take my time getting my little group on board the continental train. Usually, I had to scramble ahead to reserve seats in face of competition from the couriers of other tour groups. This time the train was virtually empty.

The journey was long and slow. Because the railway ran right down the Maginot Line, there were troops everywhere. We would travel a few miles, the train would stop and troops come on board to inspect our passports and papers. Then we would set off to have the process repeated. We eventually reached Switzerland and Sarnen on the Tuesday afternoon.

Sarnen was a different world, or so it seemed for the first day or two. The war scares were almost forgotten, for we all knew that Switzerland's tradition of neutrality was not likely to be broken. But outside that neat little Swiss world, events were moving fast.

On the Thursday the British fleet mobilised. And on Friday, September 1st, the Germans marched into Poland.

1935: *The Austrian Tyrol, pushing up the one in four hill to Seefeld (inset) repeated with son, Paul, 25 years later.*

1935: *Correctly dressed for the job in hand.*
1935: *Innsbruck, our tandem arouses interest.*

1937: *The beach at Tower Bridge, a favourite spot for East Enders in hot weather and available several hours each day at low tide.*

1939: *Lake Sarnen. Introduction of water-ski-ing to Switzerland, on a cupboard door.*

1940: *On April 27th Harry and Rene are married at Caxton Hall and depart for Torquay in Rene's new Ford 8 motor car, the first £100 car and driven off the production line at Dagenham by Rene herself.*

On Sunday, September 3rd, I walked from the Hotel Waldheim along the shore of the lake towards the tiny town. It was a bright warm day, although there was a chill in the morning air. I had heard on the hotel radio that from 11 o'clock that morning Great Britain was officially at war with Germany.

I was trying to gather my thoughts and form some plan of action. I thought about my family back in the East End, and my little group who were looking to me to get them back home, somehow or other. I had a lot on my mind as I reached the outskirts of the town and made for the main street.

It was then I realised that the place was full of troops; the prospect of war had even reached Sarnen. I did not know at first where they had all come from, but then I began to recognise the faces above the uniforms. They were the men of the town who had responded to the mobilization call and were waiting to be assigned to their war stations. I then remembered one of the hotel staff telling me the previous evening that all Swiss men keep their uniforms and their weapons at home. 'We Swiss have a precise nature,' he had joked. 'We like to be ready on time for everything, whether it is going out to dinner or preparing to fight a war. Are you as ready, over there in England?' We had laughed about that, but now yesterday had gone and the joke was over. This was reality and the men of Sarnen were no different from any other.

For most of them the parade concluded with an order to return home and remain on standby, but for some it meant orders to report to various places around the mountains, for these were honeycombed with tunnels and storage areas and other defences. It was an impressive demonstration of Switzerland's readiness, and a great contrast to our own attitude during the first weeks of the 'phoney' war.

We remained in Sarnen for the rest of the holiday, and for three or four weeks afterwards. The first practical problem was the fact that we had no money to pay for rooms or meals after September 8th, the date that under normal circumstances, we would have begun our return journey.

I had travelled over to Geneva to see the British consul and been told that a special train would be organised to take all the British in Switzerland safely back home. But as such an arrangement took time, it was likely that we would be stranded in Sarnen for at least a month.

I went to Frau Dansky, the owner of the hotel, and explained our problem. No explanations were needed, as it happened, for she was intelligent enough to realise our predicament and when, our money ran out, she agreed to extend credit to me. At least we had a roof over our heads and were not going to starve. Frau Dansky's attitude was that the war would be over by Christmas and I would be able to settle my account with her then. She did not want to risk losing my business because of the present 'little unpleasantness'!

After two or three weeks of this, one of my little group, the chap from London, came to me for advice. Instead of kicking his heels in the hotel, he had been getting out and about and had met a Swiss girl who was on holiday in Sarnen with her parents. They had all got along quite well, and the parents had invited him to return to Basle with them the next day, as their own holiday was over.

'Can you see my problem?' he asked. 'If I do go back to Basle, at least I won't be running up a hotel bill here in Sarnen, and the family seem pleased to have me go with them. But, on the other hand, I don't want to lose touch with you, because you will know when this special train is going back to Britain.'

We weighed up the problem over a couple of beers and finally decided that the best thing was for him to accept the family's invitation and travel with them to Basle. He could keep in touch with me by telephone and make his own contact with the British consulate in Geneva or in Basle (if there was one).

So off he went. He kept in touch with me as promised, and indeed he keeps in touch with me still. I get a Christmas card from him every year – from Basle. Yes, you've guessed, He married the girl and stayed in Switzerland from that day to this. They had about half a dozen children and lived happily ever after as far as I know.

The Australian chap also got tired of kicking his heels in the hotel and came up to me one morning, carrying his suitcase. 'I'm off,' he said. 'I can't hang around here any more.' Nothing I could say would dissuade him, so off he went. I worried about him for a few days, but then decided he was old enough to make his own decisions and to take care of himself.

As far as I was concerned that was the end of that and, indeed, I never heard from him and never expected to do so. However, the tailpiece to his story came one evening in November 1960 when I was walking along Piccadilly, all togged up in a dinner jacket, having attended a formal dinner. I was making my way to my London flat, when a man with an Australian accent confronted me.

'You're Harry Chandler, aren't you, mate?' he asked. I said I was, but could not recall having ever met him.

'Sarnen, 1939, mate,' he replied with a grin. 'Now d'you remember me?'

'Good God, yes,' I said. 'You got tired of waiting around and made your own way out. Whatever happened to you?'

'Nothing much. Nothing worth writing home about. But you've done pretty well for yourself, by the look of you.' We stood there for a few moments, not knowing what else to say. I had a million questions, but couldn't think of a single one. Then he clapped me on the shoulder, wished me goodnight, and walked off.

After his departure from Sarnen, I was left with a couple of people who were quite content to wait things out, and the woman I had tried to dissuade from coming. I began to get restless myself, so decided to travel to Geneva and apply at the French consulate for a visa into France. Once there, I thought I could make my way to a Channel port and get home. When I told the disabled lady my plan, she insisted on coming with me to Geneva. She did not want to be left behind and believed that somehow or other she could accompany me through unoccupied France. Off we went to Geneva and I presented myself at the French consulate the following morning, leaving the reluctant lady in her hotel room.

The street outside the consulate was crowded with people, hundreds of them, and most of them French. They, too, wanted documents to enable them to go back to their homes and, as I stood on the edge of the throng, I could see no way of getting through it and into the building. My attention was drawn to one man who was whispering urgently to one of the consulate guards or officials at the door, and I saw him pass over some money. The official vanished inside and the man remained close to the door, so I made my way over to him, asking if he was English. I had the feeling, from his bearing and his clothes, that he probably was.

And my guess was right. He admitted that he had passed over a bribe in order to get an interview ahead of the crowd, because of his special circumstances. When I raised my eyebrows at this, he said that, as a captain in the Territorial Army, he had to get back to Britain in order to report for active service.

'In that case, I'll come in with you,' I said. 'I'm in the Civil Air Guard and I've got to report as well.'

This was rather an exaggeration, but I hoped it would do the trick. In case you have never heard of it, and very few people do remember it these days, the Civil Air Guard was something they started just before the war. You joined it and went to classes and lectures on navigation. I suppose the idea was that it would form some sort of 'Territorial Air Force', or a partly trained reserve, but it never really amounted to much. How could it? It had no aircraft. However, I hoped it would be enough to get me into the French consulate with the eager TA captain.

We were eventually beckoned through the door and shown into an office, behind whose desk was an elderly Frenchman trying to remain calm under pressure. Papers were piled up all around him and he was clearly getting set for another hectic day. We introduced ourselves and the Frenchman greeted us with the offer of a cigar and a glass of brandy.

My companion of the morning took the whole thing in his stride, greeting the official with formal courtesy and making a little speech about Britain and France once more becoming allies in the fight against the Boche. 'I am a captain in the British Territorial Army and I want to return to my country so that I may fight for the liberty of France,' he declared.

At this we all raised our brandy glasses and drank a toast. The glasses were refilled and I tried to make a similar speech, ending up with 'I am a member of the Civil Air Guard and I, too, want to fight for France'. Again the glasses were drained.

Five minutes later we were back on the consulate steps with our visas in our hands and the good wishes of the emotional Frenchman ringing in our ears.

'How do you propose to reach home?' I asked the captain.

'I have a motor car, my friend,' he replied. 'And it has room for a passenger. I shall pick you up at your hotel in half an hour.'

So that was that. I hurried back to my hotel and paid my bill. My lady customer was waiting for me in the reception and burst into hysterical tears at being told that I was leaving right away. Of course, she argued that I should take her with me, but I trumped that by explaining that I had a military visa and that she was a civilian. Then she said I was deserting her, leaving her alone to face goodness knows what terrible fate. Patiently I explained that she was not alone. She could go back to Sarnen, or wait in the hotel where she was. She was registered with the British embassy, along with several hundred other British subjects in Switzerland and, in due course, would be going home in the special train.

She was still protesting when the captain drove up in his car – a huge and splendid Lagonda. There was no time for the argument to continue, so I left her on the hotel steps, waving her arms angrily, as we loaded my case into the car and drove away.

The captain was in a hurry. He had decided that we should aim to reach either Calais or Boulogne by the following day and, as it was by now late morning, there was little time to spare. He drove like a maniac to the Swiss frontier and we got through by showing our passports and our French military visas. The Swiss border guards were not too concerned about people leaving the country; they had their hands full vetting all the people hoping to get in.

Try as I may, I cannot now recall the route we took across France, except that we made sure we kept well away from the German border by swinging south-east rather than driving in a direct line for the Channel coast. I settled right down in the Lagonda's passenger seat and let the captain work out his own route, for he seemed more than capable of doing so; from one or two remarks he made, I sensed that he knew his way around Europe. Hour followed hour as night fell and the miles sped by, but as it got later, so we encountered more road blocks manned by very cautious and very jumpy French soldiers. They could hear us coming from a long way off, and were ready with raised rifles as we approached their barriers. We showed our passports and visas and were waved on without too much delay until we reached Abbeville at around three or four in the morning.

This time the soldiers at the road block decided that our passports and visas were not good enough and that, in any case, they did not like the look of us. We protested to the sergeant and to the lieutenant in charge, but were told that we would have to be detained until the major came on duty in the morning. 'But it is already morning,' I said in my best French – which was, to tell the truth, pretty awful. The sergeant replied that, for the major, the morning would not begin until eight or nine o'clock and that, in the meantime, we would have to stay right where we were.

So we made the best of it, scrounging some coffee from the guards who were, like all soldiers in such a situation, 'fed up and far from home'. We managed to create some sort of rapport with them all by the time the major arrived and fortunately, he took very little time to make his decision that we could proceed.

We sped north to cover the 80 or so kilometres to Boulogne, and did so with only the briefest of delays at a checkpoint near Montreuil. As you can imagine, the port was in a turmoil, but the captain drove down to the quay and started searching for a boat that might take us to England. I joined in the search, but did not think much of our chances in the circumstances and was about to suggest we headed on to Calais when the captain yelled at me from further down the quay and started waving his arms. Even at that distance there was no mistaking the message. He had succeeded in the search.

I hurried along and found him in the middle of haggling with the ship's captain who was about to sail for Dover. It was a scruffy old tub, fishing boat and cargo carrier all on one, but right then I would not have swapped it for the most luxurious liner. All I regretted was that the lovely Lagonda would have to be left behind. But my companion had other plans.

After much arm waving and assorted theatricals, he managed to convince the ship's captain that the car could go on board as well, for there was a convenient crane which had been used to load other cargo. The ship's captain had been dubious, but my travelling companion treated him to a variation of the speech that had worked so well in the French consulate back in Geneva, and in the end the sailor agreed.

'Right,' said the captain. 'That's going to cost us a fiver each. Do you have a fiver, Mr Chandler?' I fished around in my pockets and came up with just about enough, some English pound notes and a few Swiss francs. Then I helped to lash the Lagonda to the crane and, within half an hour, we were heading away from the harbour and over the Channel. For the first time since leaving Geneva we both felt able to relax.

We leaned on the rail, watching France recede. 'I wonder when we shall be able to go back?' I asked, half to myself.

'It will take some time,' said the captain. 'But we shall come back some day. We're going to win this one, take my word for it.'

There was a long silence and then the captain suddenly straightened up. 'I've just realised, Mr Chandler, that while you introduced yourself to me in Geneva, I have not properly reciprocated. Please forgive me. The name's Ingham. Walter Ingham.'

He held out his hand and I shook it in silence. The silence lasted for several moments, for I was trying to recover from the shock. 'Would that be Walter Ingham of Ingham's Tours?' I asked. He nodded. 'Yes, Mr Chandler. We're in the same line of business, I believe.'

It was the most incredible coincidence and one that you would never believe if somebody wrote it into the plot of a novel. Of all the people in Switzerland that I could have met, it had to be the one man whose name was already something of a legend in the fledgling holiday business.

And, just to ram that coincidence home, we ended up several years later in the same unit of the Intelligence Corps, doing Field Security work in Austria. He finished the war as a major and afterwards worked to build up the holiday company that still bears his name. He retired a dozen years ago, maybe more, and now lives on the island of Elba. Between us, I think he owns most of it!

That is the way I came home at the end of 1939, having been caught offside when the whistle blew for war. I knew, as we nosed into Dover harbour, that there would be no odd jobs to make ends meet that winter. I knew there would be no summer holiday season in 1940, with trips to the Continent . All that would have to be set aside while Herr Hitler and his lot were disposed of. And I knew that I would have to get into that fight and settle my own little personal score with the Germans who had mucked up all my plans and jackbooted all over my hopes and dreams.

At 26 years old, I was ready to go to war. But it proved more difficult to do so than I had imagined.

CHAPTER FIVE

My 'Phoney' War

THE RECRUITING office at Romford had the air of a place that had been put together in a hurry, housed temporarily in a building belonging to the local council. There were notices all over the walls and a lot of very elderly clerks filling in forms and generally bustling about. At the end of October 1939 there was no shortage of customers, and I had to wait for about half an hour before I could get up to the table and give a lot of answers to one of the clerks whose old pen scratched away like something from a Dickensian counting house.

During the wait, the group of volunteers had tried to joke among themselves, expressing their preferences for Army, Navy or Air Force, talking of their fathers' tales from 'the last lot' – the generally used description of the 1914–1918 war – and passing the time as best they could. I was one of that group and as eager as any to get into the fight. Telling the clerk of my time spent in the Civil Air Guard, I expressed a preference to serve in the RAF; within a few minutes I was sent off to another part of the building for my full medical examination.

I feared that the childhood accident which damaged my ear might affect my chances but, in the event, it was my eyesight that let me down. The RAF could not use me, so I found myself back in front of the clerk again, telling him I did not mind what I joined. Anything would do, I needed the money.

'You're 26, aren't you?' the clerk asked. A daft question, I thought, because he had my age on the form in front of him. But I said I was 26, as politely as I could. 'As things are, you're pretty close to being called up anyway,' he added. 'We are really looking for volunteers who are older and farther away from conscription. That's the routine, anyway.'

I could not work out what he was hinting at, but he soon made it very clear. Closing his little brown folder, he put it into a tray on one side of his desk. 'Go home and wait for your call up papers, Mr Chandler,' he said. 'You'll get those in two or three months!'

So that was that. But I had to do something in the meantime, not only to help the war effort, but also to earn some money. I was absolutely skint again, or as close to skint as makes no difference. The 'winding up' of my business as a holiday party organiser and travel agent had seen to that.

While I had been in Switzerland, Rene had gone round to Hermit Road from time to time to keep the paperwork in order and deal with letters. There had been a lot of correspondence from those members of the group who had decided, wisely as it turned out, to forgo their holidays. They wanted their money back, and she had written to them all that as soon as I returned from Switzerland I would communicate with them. I imagine they ail thought they had lost their money to that dodgy chap from Canning Town.

But I was determined to do right by them. As soon as I had got back I wrote to them all. I said that I wanted to tell them all what had happened, to discuss the return of their money and had arranged a meeting one Wednesday evening at the Golden Lion in Dean Street, Soho. I reserved an upstairs room, laid on a few drinks, and gave an account of my adventures in Switzerland and France. I told them that I had made out cheques for every one of them to the full amount of the ten guineas per head that I owed. At this point I held up the bundle of cheques, but added that if they all took the whole ten guineas, I would go into the red at the bank. If, however, they were prepared to settle for ten pounds, I thought I had enough to meet that – but of course the decision was up to them.

One man then said that, because I had been honest enough to meet them in this fashion and had not simply absconded with all the money, he would be prepared to take just the ten pounds. His view was shared by all the others. So I sat down at a little round table and proceeded to amend all the cheques from ten guineas to ten pounds. We then had something of a party, with the customers buying me drinks, and the evening ended on a much happier note than it had begun. But that was the end of the holiday business for me – 'for the duration' and I was still solvent – just.

Having been rejected by the recruiting office, I had to get a job. The first thing I thought of was joining the police because I had seen an advertisement appealing for volunteers. I am certainly not tall enough to be a policeman under normal circumstances but, because of the war, the usual requirements were being waived. So I went down to Canning Town police station where the sergeant filled out a couple of forms and sent me off down the road to a local GP who was apparently supposed to do all the police medicals. But, when I got there, I found he was away and his place was being taken by a locum – a lady doctor. Not knowing what was expected of her, she rang the sergeant who must have gone into great detail over the telephone. She came back into the surgery, where I was waiting in my underpants, and told me she did not feel qualified to do the job; in the end, the medical was carried out by another local doctor later that morning and it was the middle of the afternoon by the time I got back to the police station with my little piece of paper saying I was healthy enough to join the force.

It was, I remember, a Friday, and the desk sergeant was all for me starting the following Monday morning.

'Look here, mate,' I said. 'I've got absolutely no money and I want to start as soon as possible. I mean to say, you are paying £2.10s a week, aren't you?'

So he took pity on me and told me to report for duty at ten o'clock the following evening. 'There's just two things I've got to tell you,' he said, as I prepared to leave. 'First, wear a suit. Second, don't call me "mate".'

'Righto, sergeant,' I replied. 'See you tomorrow evening.'

Thinking to make a good impression, I arrived at the station a little before 10 pm, wearing a dark blue suit and trying to look 'official'. An old copper in charge of the storeroom kitted me out with a notebook, a truncheon and a whistle. He produced an armband with 'Police' on it, which I slipped over my right sleeve, and then he gave me a gasmask in a little cardboard box, and a blue tin helmet with a white 'P' painted on the front.

Along with a dozen other similarly dressed new recruits, I paraded for inspection by the sergeant. He handed out maps of the area on which our beats were marked and I saw that my beat included Greengate Street and part of Barking Road. I knew that the Green Gate public house there, just three or four hundred yards from the police station, was a pretty tough spot, especially at closing time on a Saturday night. The sergeant did not notice the apprehensive look on my face – or pretended not to – and just told us to walk our beats and return to the police station at around 2 am for a half-hour breakfast break.

I set off, very conscious of my authority, adjusting my armband every ten paces or so and patting my pockets to make sure I still had my whistle and notebook. The truncheon was stuck down my belt, inside my trouser leg, so there was no need to reassure myself of its presence!

I have been told that there is a streak in my character that makes me want to go bull-at-a-gate for anything that is ahead of me, without waiting to weigh up the pros and cons and without thinking about the things that could go wrong. I suppose it is true enough, and certainly on that Saturday evening I decided to go straight down to the Green Gate pub and take whatever was happening in my new-found stride. I had to start being a policeman sooner or later, so best make it sooner!

From quite a way off I could see, and hear, the fight that was going on as the customers poured out of the pub at closing time. That punch up on the pavement was a routine part of a Saturday night out in the East End, as the bar-room arguments took on a new lease of life in the comparatively fresh air of the Barking Road. There were two chaps wrestling and brawling around, swinging punches at each other, and a crowd egging them on.

I elbowed my way through and stepped into the fight, pushing the two men apart. They could not believe it when they saw me in my blue suit with my tin helmet and armband. 'Oh, Gawd help us,' shouted a voice from the crowd. 'It's a bloody fifty-bob-a-week copper.' Then they all joined in the 'fifty-bob-a-week' chorus, jeering and laughing and quite forgetting what the fight had been all about.

At that time everyone knew that the new recruits, the wartime constables, in their suits and armbands, were earning just fifty shillings a week, so the label was applied to them all, usually by unseen voices behind their backs as they walked the beat. But here I was, a brand new officer of the law, with a mob all around me giving me catcalls and jeers and waiting for my next move.

Frankly, I had no idea what to do until one of the two men who had been fighting decided that he did not like his evening interrupted in this fashion and swung a punch at me. Fortunately he was drunk and I could see it coming, so all he did was swing round with the force of the blow and hit the chap he was supposed to have been fighting in the first place. This chap gave him a push, then turned on me as well, telling me I had no right to interfere in a private quarrel. Then the two of them came at me, but got in each other's way and fell over.

I could see at once that one of them was too far gone to bother about getting up again, but the other staggered to his feet and launched himself in my direction. I grabbed his arm and held him up, then walked him away from the pub. He thought I was taking him home. So did the crowd. In fact, he was my first arrest.

Back at the police station the sergeant looked up in surprise as I came in with my prisoner.

'But you only started this evening,' he said. 'You've only been out five minutes. Are you trying to set a record or something?'

He came out from behind his counter, had a few sharp words with the chap I had brought in, then shoved him out through the door and on his way. 'Now listen to me,' he said very slowly, as if he was speaking to a five-year-old, 'I don't want you to go out and arrest every drunk you see on a Saturday night, because you'll fill up all our cells and we might want to use them for real criminals. Understand?'

I nodded. There was not much I could say in the face of such tremendous logic. So I went back out on my beat, determined to curb my enthusiasm.

After a couple or weeks it became clear that the 'real' police had not taken kindly to the wartime recruits and made sure that we did all the boring and routine work, leaving them free to get on with everything else. I did not fancy that idea, so determined that, when I got on to the day shift, I would take the first opportunity that came along to try my hand at doing a real policeman's work. And what better task than traffic control?

I had the spot all picked out in my mind – a notorious junction where Beckton Road joins Barking Road. It was always busy, because Beckton Road cut across into Newham Way, the A13, and drivers who knew the area used it to avoid the main junction of those roads at Silvertown Way.

So off I went, ready to show the motorists that even we 'fifty-bob-a-week' policemen could do a good job.

I took up my position, adjusted my armband, and started waving my arms about in the approved fashion. I was very strict with all the drivers, and for about a quarter of an hour it all went quite well. But it was too good to last and, when one large lorry came to a stop in the wrong place, blocking the junction completely, I realised I had created a problem I could not solve. Cars and lorries piled up all around me and when the horns started to blow I strode with great purpose around the front of the lorry that had started it all. Everyone assumed that I was going to tackle the driver but, as soon as I had got behind the vehicle and out of sight, I dodged across the Barking Road and into a side turning. Then I hurried into Hermit Road and went home for a cup of tea. I had taken on more than I could chew.

As the weeks passed into months, I settled into some sort of routine as a policeman, but there was no way of escaping the terrible boredom of the work. I would walk for hours through the deserted streets at night time, or spend day shifts on routine work. I had, at last, been kitted out with a uniform, but I was still a 'fifty-bob-a-week' copper like all the others who had joined when I had.

Apart from the family in Hermit Road, the brightest part of my life was Rene, with whom I was now 'going steady'. Although she lived over in Upminster and worked at Dagenham, we saw as much of each other as we could. I have described how she had been a real help by holding the fort for my travel business when I was stuck in Switzerland. Before the war I had not been able to see any prospect of us getting married, at least not until I had found my feet as a holiday organiser. She had a good job at Fords, earning £6 a week, which was a fortune in those days and far more than I was getting. In 1936 she had even bought herself a car – a Ford Eight which usually sold for £100 but which she got for £80 because she worked there. And not only had she bought it, but she had made a point of going into the factory and herself driving it off the end of the production line. I do not know many girls who have done that, even in this day and age of women's lib!

But, as I say, we had not been able to get married because that would have meant Rene giving up her job. Surprising as it may seem in these liberated days, married women were not allowed to work in paid employment and had to give up their jobs when they got married and we needed Rene's wages if we were going to manage. But the outbreak of war changed the entire situation. Women were being conscripted for factory and other work, and the rule about women having to leave work on marriage was cancelled.

So, in April 1940, Rene and I were married, and I moved from Hermit Road to the small flat in Springfield Court in Upminster which was to be our home through the early years of the war. I commuted between Upminster and Canning Town police station on my motor bike, 'doing my bit' for the war effort, but realising as the months passed that, for me, my kind of police work was utterly boring and depressing.

Like Air Raid Wardens and others who had been 'dressed in a little brief authority' at the outbreak of war, the fifty-bob-a-week coppers were treated with contempt by some, and with indifference by most. There was always the assumption that, by joining the police or becoming a warden, a man had somehow dodged his real responsibilities and was avoiding service in the forces. A lot of air raid wardens were, in fact, too old to serve, but all were tarred with the same brush. During the months of what was called 'the phoney war' the majority of people had not understood what all the fuss was about. They could not take the situation seriously, and they could not take the wardens and the police seriously either.

Then the bombs began to fall.

That summer of 1940 had seen the evacuation from Dunkirk and the collapse of France, bringing the Germans right up to our doorstep on the other side of the Channel. And even to the military occupation of the Channel Islands. Anybody who followed the war news was all too well aware of the next step in the German routine of conquest – a long succession of bombing raids to soften up the target for invasion. It had worked that way for Hitler every time, and he was sure to try it on us, for all that the Channel was no easy border to cross. The raids on London began that summer, towards the end of August. In September, they grew worse. The phoney war was over.

As the bombs fell the East End of London took the brunt of it. The winter of 1940–41 was a winter of horror, but in typical British fashion the East Enders took the German name for it, and used it as our own. 'The Blitz' became an English expression.

Early one morning in May 1941, I reported as usual to Canning Town police station at the start of my duty shift. A quarter to six, it was, and I was due to remain on duty until two in the afternoon, or maybe even later. You could never tell what each day would bring.

The previous night London had suffered one of the heaviest air raids of the war. Over 1500 people had been killed and Canning Town had copped more than its fair share. The desk sergeant was busy assigning constables to the various scenes of 'incidents', as the jargon called them – it was a nice, sterile, civil service word to describe a hole in the ground where a row of houses had once stood, and where bodies were being dug from the rubble. Anyway, I was assigned to my 'incident' and set off, realising that the route would take me along Hermit Road. I could pop my head round the door and wish the family good morning, I thought.

But as I walked down Hermit Road, I realised that here, too, there had been an 'incident' the night before. A great part of the street had simply disappeared into an enormous crater.

The rescue service men were still there, shifting beams and masonry and digging through the ruins. My home, number 25, had been right in the middle of it.

I tried to help with the digging but, in truth, I was more of a hindrance than a help, so I set about finding out just what had happened. It transpired that a landmine had wiped out the whole street during the night. My family would have been taking shelter under the stairs when it fell; they always went under the stairs when the sirens sounded.

As I arrived, they were digging out my youngest brother, Arthur. He died as they were lifting him clear, and they gently laid his body down and covered him with a blanket. He was 14 years old. With other schoolchildren he had been evacuated to the country, but had returned home three or four weeks previously because he had missed his home and his family. This was his homecoming.

My stepmother was brought out – dead – and then my sister, Olive. The remarkable thing about her was that she was not even bruised. She must have been sheltered by the body of my stepmother above her. All her clothes had been blown or torn off, and she was covered in black soot and brick dust. But there was not even the slightest scratch on her. As she sat wrapped in blankets, I asked the rescuers about my father, the only other member of the family in the house when the landmine dropped as my brother Bill was in the army. One of the rescue team said he had been got out just before I arrived. Alive or dead? He did not know, he said, because he had been some distance away. But I should be prepared for the worse.

I hurried back to Canning Town police station to report all this to the sergeant. First, however, I got a message to Irene, who drove over from Upminster to collect Olive. She took her to our little flat, gave her a hot bath and put her to bed. Olive was physically untouched by the experience, but you cannot go through something like that without scars on the soul, and these she carried for a long time afterwards. However, she recovered well enough to join the ATS and served on an anti-aircraft gun-site in Hyde Park commanded by Winston Churchill's daughter Mary.

At the police station, the sergeant told me to go off in search of my father, knowing that I was fit for nothing else that day. This meant doing the rounds of the mortuaries which had been set up in the local public baths. The huge swimming pools had been emptied and hundreds of metal trays fitted into them. Bodies brought out of bombed houses were taken to the baths and laid on trays with covering blankets. It was a gruesome business, going along with all the other grieving people, lifting the blankets in search of a relative.

You can imagine that people were terribly upset by this, and there was a lot of crying and wailing going on, but what really made my blood boil was a big notice painted up on one end of the pool area. 'Do not scream and shout', it said, which I found really callous. I imagined that some petty unfeeling official had had it put up because of the noise the grieving people were making. It was just the sort of thing you expected from some of these people – 'Little Hitlers' we called them – because they had wangled soft jobs in order to dodge military service and liked to throw their weight about.

Anyway, that notice really upset me and it was not until many years later that I realised how wrong my assumptions had been. The notice had dated from the time when the swimming baths were being used for their proper purpose, and was to be found in all pools, aimed at young and excited children whose boisterous noise could hide the sound of someone in trouble calling for help.

I checked the tin trays in three or four baths and then made my way back to the sergeant to tell him I had not found my father's body. 'You won't find him in a mortuary, because he's not dead,' said the sergeant. 'I've been trying to get in touch with you to tell you he was brought out alive. He's been injured and taken to hospital in Barnet.'

I was overjoyed at this news. 'I'll get round there right away, sergeant,' I said, 'Which hospital is he in?' 'They've taken him to Colney Hatch,' replied the sergeant. 'But don't jump to the wrong conclusion because it isn't being used as a lunatic asylum now. It's been converted into a casualty hospital.'

My father had been very badly injured; he had lost an eye and had to have a leg amputated. He had also damaged his lungs and was in a terrible state when they got him out of the wreckage, so it was no wonder that the rescue chap had thought he might be dead.

Other people had also jumped to that conclusion. He was a member of a local billiards club and a day or two after the bombing some of his friends came to see me at the police station. They had assumed everybody had been killed and wanted to know when the funeral would be held. When I told them he was still alive, they were quite taken aback. 'But we had a collection for a wreath,' said one of them. I think he was quite annoyed that my father had put them to all that trouble for nothing!

On one of my visits to see him in Colney Hatch, I told him about this and we laughed it off. But at the end of a year or so, when he got out of hospital, he went round to the billiards club and asked for the wreath money! They gave him the results of the collection, quite a considerable sum I believe and he spent the evening treating his mates in the club in celebration of his return from the dead.

Shortly afterwards the bombing eased off and, as the weeks of 1941 passed by, my conviction increased that the police force was not for me. It was no good my waiting for the call up, because the police service had been designated a 'reserved' occupation which meant that I was now exempt from conscription. I had in fact tried to enlist a couple more times, but the recruiting people would have nothing to do with me once they learned of my occupation. But as the bombing had eased, I felt I was once again fighting that 'phoney' war, and certainly did not intend to be stuck in Canning Town for the duration, for it had become the most depressing place imaginable as you will see from the picture on page 00. I spent eight hours every night trudging round these desolate ruins alone and not seeing a soul. In the early morning I went home to our small flat in Upminster to go to bed just as Rene was getting up to go to work at Fords, and in the evening I went to Colney Hatch to visit my father who was to remain a whole year in hospital enduring many operations with incredible fortitude.

Conditions were made worse during the late summer of 1941 because huge parts of the East End had been evacuated and Canning Town had become just row after row of empty bomb and shell holes, with a few buildings here and there – an absolute no man's land. Many people had moved out to Epping Forest when the bombing started, and had remained there, living in tents or making huts for themselves out of anything that came to hand. It was amazing how quickly a so called civilised society could revert to such conditions, and how easily the people adapted to them, travelling into work from their huts and tents every morning, just as if they were commuting from their ordinary homes.

That was merely one aspect of East End life during those months of the Blitz and its aftermath. There were others, which did not get much attention at the time, for obvious reasons of morale, and which have not been given much attention since because the accepted version of events is that all East Enders bore themselves bravely under the onslaught and kept their 'cheery Cockney humour' intact. According to the history books, we were all supposed to be real little warriors, defying the might of the Hun, helping each other out and anxious to fight back as soon as the opportunity came. The truth was sometimes very different.

Oh, there was bravery and fortitude all right, and many people discovered a strength of character they had not known they possessed. But there was another side to the East End, and as a policeman I encountered it.

There were, for example, the Silvertown Way arches. Before the war this road had been built from Canning Town and Barking Road into the docks, and had been raised over existing roads and buildings by a series of arches. As soon as the bombing began, most of the arches were taken over as air raid shelters with primitive sleeping facilities but no sanitation. A lot of men ended up living there, the women and children having been evacuated from the bombs. These men were, in the main, the worst possible types you can imagine. Drunks and drop-outs and petty criminals, terrified of the bombs and scrambling around the ruins of the neighbourhood, scavenging and stealing rather than doing any kind of useful work. The arches were infested with them and the whole place stank to high heaven. We were supposed to go down there from time to time because it was the obvious bolt-hole for anybody wanted by the police, but I hated to do that because I could not stand the awful stench. I had read, as a schoolboy, about the 'stews' of London in the days of Dickens, where the criminals gathered and no honest man dared to walk:

the kind of filthy back alleys in which Fagin taught his pickpockets. I never thought I would encounter such conditions in the twentieth century, but the arches under Silvertown Way were just that. As I say, it is an aspect of wartime London that was ignored by the press at the time because it did not fit into the propaganda picture. But it existed all right.

As if that had not been enough, we also had to contend with packs of wild dogs that appeared on the scene. When people decamped to Epping Forest or were evacuated to other parts of the country, they mostly left their pets behind; after a couple of weeks the dogs would begin to revert to their wild instincts, forming packs of ten, twenty or thirty animals and ranging around the bombsites in search of food. With hardly anything to eat, they became bolder and dangerous, invading those areas where people were still living. Something had to be done, so the RSPCA were called in. They brought rifles and we drew pistols from the police station store – provided under wartime emergency regulations. We then simply went out and, for several days, shot on sight every dog we came upon. I am not sentimental about animals, and I knew the job had to be done, but it was hard going. It was certainly not what I had anticipated when I joined the police, so I redoubled my efforts to get into the army.

It was no use trying at the local recruiting office because all they did was tell me what a wonderful and useful job I was doing as a policeman. So, knowing I had nothing to lose, I wrote direct to the War Office.

I enclosed with the letter a number of photographs I had taken in Berlin and Hamburg during my trips with Albert. I remember one in particular was of Berlin railway station festooned with swastika banners. I said I had more pictures of German troops and police, and of other places I had been. I also said I knew Germany pretty well and spoke the language fluently.

Four days later I received a reply, giving me the name of the man I should see at the War Office and fixing a day and time for the appointment. I duly presented myself, along with my portfolio of photographs, which seemed to interest this chap no end. He established that I spoke fluent German – and by this time it *was* fluent – and also that I wanted to leave the police force. After a few more questions he scribbled a name and address on a slip of paper and passed it to me.

'Write to this man,' he said. 'I shall speak to him and he will be expecting a letter from you. If he decides that the army needs you, there will be no obstacle to your leaving the police service. I don't imagine you get much opportunity of practising your German in Canning Town these days?' He smiled as he asked the question. 'I don't think it would be good for my health to walk around the East End speaking German,' I replied. 'But it does seem a pity to let it go to waste.'

I went away and wrote the letter, as instructed, and about a week later I was called for a second interview with a major who looked and spoke like a university don. It was in a rather mysterious, closely guarded premises on the top floor of St Ermin's Hotel, Westminster, next door to

1937: *In the Austrian Tyrol, Harry Chandler as courier with his client Irene Ellis, later his wife.*

1936: *The Battle of Cable Street. The Police try to force a passage for Sir Oswald Moseley, Leader of the British Union of Fascists, to address 3,000 blackshirts assembled at the Tower of London. Huge crowds estimated at 100,000 had collected along the route of the march and 7,000 police were brought into the area, including the entire mounted corps of the Metropolitan Police. A vivid memory of my first experience of violence in the streets.*

Caxton Hall where I had been married a couple of years before. We spoke German for a few minutes, then he reverted to English and asked where I had learned the language. I told him. 'Ah, you're a night school chap are you?' he asked. 'Would you say you've got an inquiring mind?'

I thought I had, but had to say that I had not had a university education or degrees. His next question really surprised me. 'Do you play bridge? Or chess?' I told him that I did, and he pondered on that for a little while. Although I did not realise it at the time, some inquiries must have been made about me, so the major knew more about my background than he was letting on.

In the end he got up from behind his desk and showed me to the door. 'You'll be hearing from us, Mr Chandler,' he said. 'I don't think you will have too long to wait for your transfer out of the police force.'

He was right. At the beginning of October 1941, I received my orders to join the army. Without knowing exactly how or why, I had been recruited into Military Intelligence. MI5, no less.

CHAPTER SIX

In at the Deep End

I N VIEW of all the glamour that surrounds Military Intelligence and the times novels and films have featured brave secret agents risking all for their country and gathering beautiful girls along the way, in view of all that, I think you ought to know right away that it was not a case of 007 Chandler, licensed to kill and sent off to do away with the Führer. Nor was I given a top secret briefing and parachuted into Berlin on a specially adapted tandem!

No, I was sent to King Alfred's College in Winchester. To the Guards Training Depot. The army clearly had its priorities sorted out and, before you could be a spy, you had to learn how to polish a pair of boots and to salute smartly. Actually, there was no question of me being a spy, as you will learn as I unfold my brilliant military career for your inspection. What I had to do was get used to the army's way of doing things and, as far as the Guards were concerned, there was only one way – the best.

What had apparently happened at the outbreak of war was that most members of Military Intelligence, although undeniably clever and well suited for the work, had no idea of military discipline and wartime conditions. Many had been issued with motor cycles for example, resulting in scores of casualties because they had not known how to ride the wretched things.

'The army has decided that this will not happen again,' we were told by one of the lecturers on our very first day. 'The army was decided that you will first learn to be good soldiers. You will learn army discipline. You will learn to obey orders and salute smartly. We shall teach you the army way of riding a motor cycle, so you don't kill yourselves like so many of your predecessors.'

He went on to list the myriad things that would await us during the course of our indoctrination into the army. Anybody who has served in the armed forces will know, pretty well, what we went through.

We were drilled by sergeants from the Guards, and when they teach drill, it stays taught. I do not think I measured up to their exacting standards, but I very soon realised that, as with any other large organisation, the best thing to do was to keep your head down and keep out of trouble. I marched up and down, right turned, left turned and about turned, and did everything I was told, if not perfectly, then at least with a show of eagerness. I only got caught out doing something wrong on one occasion, and the punishment was pack drill – marching at the double 'AT THE DOUBLE!!!' around the parade ground carrying full pack and rifle. Once was enough.

When it came to learning how to ride a motor bike, I thought I was well ahead of the game because I had been a keen motor cyclist for years. I imagined this would be the easy part of the course, because so many of the others had no idea at all. Once again I was proved wrong, for I had underestimated how the army set about doing such things. Faced with the task of teaching a bunch of soldiers how to ride a motor bike, the army simply recruited professional dirt track riders to do it. Motor bike racing was tremendously popular in the 1920s and 1930s, far more so than it is today, and these professional riders were brilliant. It took me about half an hour to conclude that I only *thought* I could ride a motor bike, and another ten seconds to conclude that I would never be as good as they were. But they were able to polish up my performance to meet army requirements, so that was all right.

I felt really sorry for most of the people on the course with me. They were well educated linguists, university graduates and other intellectual types. One, I recall, was a member of the Rothschild family. They inhabited a different world and found it most difficult to adapt to the army way. In addition, there was an enormous number of cranks and eccentrics who had filtered into intelligence as the war went on. We were described as the lunatic fringe of the army and I, for one, would not have quarrelled with that.

At the end of three months – in fact, at the end of the 1941 – I was posted to an Intelligence Training Centre at Smedleys Hydro in Buxton, Derbyshire for a few weeks in order to learn the rudiments of code breaking. I was assigned to what was called the 'Y' service, a section of MI6. It was all very top secret, with headquarters in Broadway, near where New Scotland Yard is now located. I would not have minded being posted there. But the army sent me to Frinton-on-Sea.

Basically, the work consisted of wireless interception. A powerful receiver was installed in the rear of a Humber Super Snipe, the fastest car that the army had at the time, and the operator tuned in to messages that were passing between German tank formations over in Holland. There was a lieutenant in charge, a driver, a wireless operator and a corporal whose task was to read the messages and break down the codes. I was that corporal. The only fly in the ointment was my striking lack of success as a code breaker. I told the officer in charge that I was no good, but he said I should stick to it and it would all come to me. He was the sort of chap who took everything the army supplied – and everyone, too – without thinking for a moment that the army might have got it wrong, as they certainly had in my case.

I remember asking him one day why we had to dash around the countryside in our Super Snipes lying in ditches in the rain all night. Why did we not stay in one place and tune in to the Germans? His reply sums up his entire philosophy. 'Corporal, a 'Y' service unit is classified as a front line unit. Front line units are issued with Super Snipe vehicles. Your unit, therefore, has a Super Snipe, and must make full use of it. Is that clear?'

What can you say in the face of such devastating logic?

I stuck to this for a while until we got posted to a place near Bishop's Stortford, which nobody in their right mind could call a front line location. So they took away our cars and we spent most of our time in the stables of some country mansion, sitting up all night trying to de-code these messages. I was just as hopeless as I had been at Frinton.

As we had a lot of time on our hands, I asked one day if I might have permission to ride and exercise the horses that were kept at this country place. The owners – an old man and his wife, rattling round in the mansion like a pair of peas in a colander – refused point blank to consider such a request. They wanted nothing to do with us and certainly did not want us invading their home or riding their horses. Considering the circumstances, it was a pretty terrible attitude to adopt. We had not been sent there by choice, and although we did not want them to look upon us as the salt of the earth, defending them from the Evil Hun, neither did we much like being regarded as 'those bloody army louts down in the paddock'.

We encountered the same attitude in the local village. They turned their backs on us in the pub as if we had been an occupying army of foreigners, and in a way I suppose that is what we were to these village people.

It was pretty depressing all round but, early in 1943 I was transferred from the 'Y' service into Field Security. All I can say about Field Security is that if you ever have the misfortune to be shoved into a war, the best thing you can do is to get into Military Intelligence. If, having done that, you get another choice, then get into Field Security. Because in Field Security you do not always have to wear a uniform and nobody knows what you are doing – in fact, neither do you, most of the time.

In April 1943, just before my 30th birthday, I was posted, as a member of a Field Security Unit, to Egypt. As I understood it at the time, we and all the others who sailed out with us were to help reinforce Montgomery at Tobruk. But we got there too late – and that was about par for the course as far as my army career was concerned. I was supposed to be in five or six different invasions, but all were cancelled, aborted at the last minute or simply failed. Or, in the case of the big one, I was given something else to do, again at the last minute.

Our late arrival in Tobruk was due to having had to come the long way round. We had sailed from Avonmouth on the *Bergensfjord*, a tiny Norwegian freighter which had about 2,000 men on board. We were packed into five or six decks, sleeping in hammocks, and living in conditions that even now I shudder to recall. That voyage is imprinted on my memory not only because it coloured my attitude towards the British army for a very long time, but also because it sowed the seeds of my political opinions for many years afterwards. I had a few revolutionary ideas which came to the surface when we were on that trip, and I was within a hair's breadth of being charged with mutiny.

We were not told our destination, of course, although most of the men on board believed that, as 'privileged' members of Field Security, we did know. We did not disillusion them, and went about looking suitably mysterious and keeping a careful note of the direction in which we sailed. To our surprise after sailing north to Scotland, we headed due west for three or four days.

Leaning on the rail one evening, I had a quiet conversation with a fellow member of the unit. We had been trying to fathom out our destination and had decided that, for reasons best known to itself, the army was sending us to the United States of America. We reckoned we were not heading far north enough for it to be Canada, although there was a possibility we might veer south and end up in the West Indies! All this finely tuned geographical knowledge was based on school atlases, dimly remembered. Unfortunately, our conversation was overheard, and within a couple of hours the rumour had spread through the ship that we were heading for New York!

After a few days, however, we turned south and, later, headed east. The great sweep out into the Atlantic had been a maneouvre to avoid submarines patrolling the western approaches.

We were in a very slow convoy and, as the time passsed, the mental attitude of the men began to change. Some began to crack up, withdrawing into themselves and brooding in silence for hours or, at the other extreme, flaring up into a terrible temper at the slightest provocation, or at no provacation at all. There was nothing for any of us to do as the days dragged past. Nothing at all.

The ship was so crowded that there was hardly room to move. There were queues for everything. One queue lasted for 12 hours a day when the NAAFI was open, with men buying tins of fruit to eat because the food was inedible. Within a week the NAAFI had run out of everything. There was an enormous queue for the temporary toilets and an awful stench from them. They were so foul that the whole ship smelled. That, added to the wretched smell of seasick soldiers, just made the entire experience worse. I got seasick like everyone else, but worked out that the best thing to do was get into the lavatory queue when it was shortest – at about two or three in the morning. So I used to get out of my hammock and queue for about half an hour to use the lavatory, then go over and wait in the queue for drinking water.

This was when I began to get rebellious. I thought there must be something terribly wrong with the British army if it had to treat its men in such a way. Looking back, the circumstances were probably due to the pressures of that particular period of the war when casualties at sea were very high.

Eventually the *Bergensfjord* reached Freetown, in Sierra Leone, 'the white man's grave', I believe they used to call it. Well, it might have been for all we knew, because not a single one of us set foot ashore, although we sat for three weeks in Freetown harbour. We were told that enemy submarines were patrolling the coast, just waiting to pick us off, and that we were remaining in harbour until they ran short of fuel and had to head back to their base.

Our only distraction was watching the natives dive off a raft tied alongside the ship to catch coins we threw into the water, providing they were silver. I remember a dozen or so heaving on a rope to salvage bales of cotton floating in the sea; when they had nearly got the bale to the deck, someone would throw a couple of silver coins overboard. Two or three immediately let go of the rope and dived for the coins. As the others were hesitating, the weight proved too much for them and back the bale fell into the water. It was worth hearing their lurid language when they discovered the silver coins were halfpennies covered with silver paper.

Eventually we left Freetown and headed south, making for a South African port. By then everyone on board knew that we would have to call at South Africa, though there was little chance of this being our final destination. Just which port we were making for was supposed to remain a secret, although after a day or two we members of the Field Security Unit were told that it was to be Durban.

We were also told to give the men lectures and instructions about security – how to watch out for strangers in bars and keep their mouths shut about our final destination, and so on. As none of them knew what the final destination was to be, there seemed little point in telling them to keep quiet about it, but I had learned not to argue with the system and so dutifully gave the lectures. Before long, everyone on the ship knew that Durban would be our port of call. And everyone thanked the Lord that we would at last be free from this dreadful ship and have some time ashore.

We sailed into Durban early one morning, all eager for the order to disembark. That had been scheduled for 10 am. As we got closer to the quayside I could see a woman singing at us with all her might. She was the legendary 'Silver Lady of Durban' who greeted all the troopships in this fashion; after all these years it might seem corny and sentimental, but I remember that her songs had most of us crying like babies.

We were still full of emotion when the order came to gather up our kit and disembark in full marching order. We paraded in rank upon rank all along the quayside, were briefly inspected, then ordered to march out. Off we went, swinging along with a fair amount of enthusaism and expecting to end up in barracks where at least the beds would not rock around all night and where, perhaps, the food might be a little more edible. As we marched, we speculated on how long we would spend in Durban. Days or weeks? Maybe two or three months. Who could tell?

After almost two hours of marching, I realised that we had virtually swung around in a great circle and were heading back for the docks. Surely, not even the army could play such a cruel trick? But the army could, and the army did. The *Bergensfjord* had gone, but another ship was waiting to take us all on board. Another ship just as small and just as awful. In the middle of the afternoon she sailed away from Durban and we were back in the same conditions as before.

The ship made her way slowly north-east, along the African coast, heading for the Horn of Africa, the Gulf of Aden and, we now realised, the Red Sea and Egypt. The lack of activity on board, the routine of queueing and the whole awful boredom began to take their toll once more.

Late one afternoon I saw a man fall (or maybe jump) overboard. I raised the alarm, only to be told by ship's officer to keep quiet and not to disturb the other men; because of the submarine threat, the ship would not stop to pick anyone up, much less go about to search for a man in the sea. There was no point in drawing attention to a man overboard under those circumstances, he pointed out. He would advise the naval escort, and that was the end of it.

The heat during the day was almost unbearable, with each morning starting very warm and the temperatures quickly building up. The sea – the Indian Ocean – rolled on relentlessly. It seemed we would spend the rest of our lives in these conditions.

At this stage of the journey most of us were sleeping out in the open on deck. Every inch of the ship was covered in bodies, but I found a place where I could sleep undisturbed – on a plank beside one of the lifeboats some six feet above the deck. The plank was about 18 inches wide and I found that, if I wedged myself up there and kept rigid, I could sleep. There was, admittedly, the risk that I would go overboard if the ship rolled badly, but I took the chance and spent hours and hours on my little plank, either asleep or dozing.

What made the experience worse was the evident discrepancy between the unsavoury conditions we had to endure and the comfort in which the officers lived. On the top deck were the quarters for the ship's captain and his officers and in these and other cabins the army officers on board – 30 or 40 of them – were enjoying more or less peacetime conditions. The sort of conditions you would get on a cruise ship.

Up there, fighting for a few inches of deck space or clinging to my little plank, I could look through the portholes and see them in their dress uniforms, eating and drinking, being waited on and having a jolly good time. The rest of the men could see this, too, and it made for a lot of resentment in our lice ridden conditions.

As corporal, I was in charge of one table on the mess deck and when, at a dinner, the officer of the day asked if there were any complaints, I snapped to attention and said 'Yes Sir'. Now this was unheard of – like Oliver Twist asking for more – and the sergeants and warrant officer crowded round in a very menacing fashion. I was anxious not to spoil my case by losing my temper, so I kept very calm, very respectful, very correct, and asked for permission to make a protest. I had to go through a whole lot of rigmarole, but eventually was marched into the CO's office (at 'double time' of course, for that was all part of the army's lunacy) and proceeded to 'state my grievance'.

I listed my complaints about the constant queueing, the state of the food, the lavatories and the generally bad conditions. At this point the CO asked me if I was making the complaint on my own behalf or whether I was speaking for others. This was the Catch-22, because I had to reply that I was speaking only for myself. Some barrack-room lawyer had told me that, if I claimed to be speaking on behalf of others, this would amount to 'rebellious conduct'. As soon as he heard my reply, the CO pointed out, quite reasonably, that others were suffering the same conditions without complaining. So that was the end of that.

But to give him his due, I think he had listened and had taken particular note of my remark that, because of the conditions the men were having to endure, their hatred and resentment was being turned away from the Hun and towards the army and our own officers. The ship was breeding rebellion because of the enormous difference in privilege between the ranks and the officers.

As you may imagine, my gesture made not the slightest difference to the conditions on board, and we sweltered on towards our destination. In the middle of June 1943, we arrived at Suez, too late for the purpose for which we had been sent, which was the invasion of Sicily, now accomplished without our assistance.

We travelled overland from Suez to Cairo and ended up in a large camp at Helwan to the south of the city. The first thing we discovered was that we could buy eggs from the locals, as the Egyptians raised a peculiar breed of tiny chicken which seemed to live off grains of sand! The eggs were small, but they were a luxury after life at sea. The second thing I discovered was that the pyramids were close by, So I went off to see them at the very first opportunity. I have seen these ancient wonders of the world several times since, but I shall never forget the first impact they made on me all those years ago. This was really foreign – far more so than France or Germany or Switzerland.

Although we were there for a long time, and took the opportunity of going to the pyramids and into Cairo itself, strangely there were people in the camp who did not stir beyond the gate. While they claimed to be bored and certainly appeared to be so they were not prepared to shift themselves and see the sights. Human nature does not change: I have often heard people on holiday complain about being bored and yet making no effort at all to get out and about.

As the weeks went by we sat around at Helwan, occupying our tents and occupying our time as best we could. By now I was a member of what was called the 98 Special Field Security Section, consisting of a dozen corporals, a sergeant-major and an officer, and the driver of a truck. We had BSA 500cc motor bikes and had been assigned a task in the event of an invasion by British forces on territory occupied by the enemy. We would be supplied with black lists and white lists and our orders were to round up the people on the black list and give assistance to those on the white. I assumed that the people on the black list would be put into prison or maybe bumped off, but the officer would be the only one holding the lists, so that was his problem.

One day a chap from HQ in Cairo had come drifting through Helwan and made a point of stopping by our tents to pass the time of day. He had asked if we were finding enough to occupy our time and suggested that, if not, we should learn a foreign language. 'You might find Italian would come in useful,' he had said, giving us a knowing look.

With that as a spur, several members of the section had started to brush up on their Italian and soon it was an open secret that we were pre-paring for an invasion of either Sicily or the Italian mainland. Several more weeks went by with no official indication of our move but, one morning, an officer came over to the tents and told us to be ready to move out within half an hour. That's the army for you – leaves you sitting around for a couple of months, then expects you to be off in 30 minutes. 'So it's Italy is it?' asked one of the corporals. 'Good Lord no,' said the officer. 'You're going to Palestine.'

He darted off, leaving us looking at each other in sheer bewilderment. Either the chap from HQ had been working a clever bluff when he suggested learning Italian or, more likely, he had neither known nor probably meant anything by his suggestion. Either way, we were on the move again.

We struck out from Helwan in a convoy with the lorry leading and the motor bikes trailing along but, as soon as we left the buildings behind and the dust started to rise, we motor cyclists got ahead of the lorry and headed out across the Sinai Desert. It was a barren landscape and, to tell the truth, a little bit frightening, but at least we were travelling together and that made it seem better.

After three hours or thereabouts my bike stopped. I fiddled with it and managed to get it going, trying to keep up with the other bikes, but it would not work properly and stopped again. I stood at the side of the track, watching the other bikes disappearing in a cloud of dust and small pebbles, and waiting for the lorry to catch me up. I figured I could sling the bike in the back and hitch a lift, but the officer had other ideas. The truck driver (who, naturally, knew more about motor bikes than any of us motor cyclists) diagnosed some fault or other and said I could ride it, but would have to keep stopping to let it cool down. I suggested hitching a lift, but this was vetoed by the officer. If the bike could be ridden, it would be ridden, he said and that was the end of that. Corporal Chandler could use his initiative and make his own way to Tel Aviv. Goodbye Corporal Chandler.

So there I was, in the middle of the Sinai Desert, trying to follow a rough track marked by stones on a motor bike that kept stopping. The sun was so hot that the bike would not cool off, even when I managed to drag it into a patch of shade. The 'cooling off' pauses got longer and longer as the sun began to dip and I was beginning to get very worried indeed. I had finished off my rations and the last of the water, and was just beginning to have visions of dying in the desert when I saw what I thought was a mirage – a great grey shape bobbing in the sky a couple of miles ahead. I stared hard at it, then turned away. When I looked back I fully expected it to have vanished, but there it still was, bobbing away.

I mounted my not so trusty steed and limped along in the direction of the shape. As it got bigger and more solid, I knew it was no mirage. It was a barrage balloon, floating high above the empty desert. If I made my way to where it was tethered, there was every chance I would find somebody.

And I did. The balloon winch was mounted on the back of an RAF truck parked in the desert. Beside it was a small tent and, sitting outside on a couple of canvas chairs, were two airmen. As I rode up, they greeted me without any sign of surprise, offered me a mug of tea and invited me to share their rations. I could smell the eggs frying and they told me, as we ate, that they had bought them from a bunch of Arabs who had pitched their own tents about a quarter of a mile away.

As we sat under the black night sky ablaze with a billion brilliant stars, I discovered that they had been living in their little tent for just over a year, but did not know exactly why they were there. They kept the balloon flying and, if it got a puncture or was damaged, they brought it down, repaired it, and then put it up again. On being asked how they managed for rations, for fags and mail and gas for the balloon, they explained that every three weeks or thereabouts a truck came through and dropped off whatever they had ordered on the previous occasion. I pressed them for an explanation but they quite genuinely could not give me one. There was nothing for the balloon to be defending and all I could assume was that it was being flown as a beacon of some kind – a navigation aid. But that was only a guess. The two men seemed quite content, and were obviously getting through a lot of library books! They were not even curious about what was happening to the war that had brought them there. It was, to say the least, a bizarre encounter.

Next morning I worked for a while on the bike, then gingerly rode off across the desert. From that day to this I have never found out what they had been doing out there. Knowing the way the services operate, I would not be at all surprised if they were still there!

Eventually I reached an ordnance depot, again situated in the middle of nowhere, and reported to the CO that I was a member of 98 Special

Field Security Unit, anxious to get to Tel Aviv for military reasons that I was not at liberty to divulge. This impressed him no end. Well, anything would have, because he and his unit were twiddling their thumbs, forgotten by everybody, and my arrival was the highspot of their week – or possibly their month. He handed me over to a sergeant mechanic who fell on the bike and proceeded to tear it apart in order to fix the fault. In the end he took me back to the CO, reported that the bike was beyond repair – which it certainly was by the time he was finished with it – and recommended that I be issued with the replacement from store. And yes, they had plenty of bikes in store for me to choose from, all in absolutely pristine condition and waiting in the middle of the desert for goodness knows what reason. I signed the appropriate chit and exchanged my old bike for a new one, then set off on my journey. Three days later I reached Tel Aviv.

It did not take me long to find my unit and report. The officer in charge said I was to hold myself in readiness for instant action as we would be moving off at any moment. Knowing the way the army worked by now, all the members of the unit took this as a sign that we would be spending quite a long time in Tel Aviv. I forget exactly how long it was, but we had time to visit Haifa and other sights, and spent several afternoons and evenings in the places run by the WVS where you could get a nice cup of tea and chat to the ladies about home. Although I did not realise it at the time, that brief encounter with the WVS in Tel Aviv must have planted the seed of an idea that was to bear fruit a couple of years later.

It looked as if were were going to hang around just like in Cairo, but then one evening the order came to move out of camp with all our gear and get to the airport. It was time for Chandler to take part in an invasion – the first of several that did not happen as planned. As we waited around the airport, we learned that the island of Kos, occupied by the Italian army, had been captured by our naval forces and that the first wave of aircraft had gone in carrying troops to defend it against any German counter-attack. Our role was to go in with the second wave, equipped with our motor bikes and our famous black and white lists. Why we had to do this from Tel Aviv I have no idea, but that was the plan.

It did not work out. The Germans retook the island and captured or killed the troops who had flown in. There was no part for us to play so, after hanging around the airport for a while, we were ordered back to camp. A couple of days later we were told that we would be going all the way back to Cairo. I did not much relish the idea of making that journey again on the motor bike despite the prospect of visiting the two RAF chaps with their balloon, but the army transported us by train. Freight train.

We loaded the bikes into one truck and clambered into another, sitting and squatting on the metal floor for the long trip back. The journey took something like 48 hours, with the train travelling at hardly more than walking pace – or so it seemed. The floor was rock hard and the sand got in everywhere!

Life back in Helwan was just as excruciatingly boring as it had been first time round – after all, you can only visit the pyramids so many times before they become familiar. I have re-read some of the letters I wrote to Rene at the time and am inclined to agree with her that I was pretty close to going off my head.

In one letter I related in detail the habits of the desert ants that I had been observing. A dozen or so of us shared a small tent where we were stuck for months with nothing whatever to do, so I had begun to study the ants which came out of a hole near the tent and wandered off across the desert in a jagged line that stretched for one or two miles. They were all carrying little bits of stuff – tiny twigs, pieces of sand and Lord knows what else. I followed this line to its destination: another little hole all that distance away. What was even more remarkable – and I swear this is true – there was not a single ant to be seen on Sundays. They were six-day-a-week ants!

Our boredom was broken suddenly and unexpectedly again with orders to travel immediately to Palestine. This time, however, we travelled by train all the way to Haifa and stayed for a few quite comfortable and interesting weeks. We had our motor cycles and were issued with civilian suits and with the most prized possession I ever had in the army – a pass signed by the General Officer Commanding, Middle East Forces, which gave Corporal Chandler his express permission to be in any place within the Palestinian theatre of operations at any time in or out of uniform. The idea appeared to be that we would frequent the local bars and markets keeping our ears open for information about the Jews from Arab sources, and vice versa, in view of the tense situation between them in Palestine. We took it, however, as a general permission to take a few weeks holiday, riding our motor bikes all over Palestine, spending a lot of time sunbathing on the beaches and visiting the Kibbutzim.

After a few weeks this very pleasant interlude was shattered by the arrival of another one of those top secret and immediate orders to move back to Cairo and Helwan by rail. The bitterest blow was the withdrawal of our precious passes and our return to uniform, military discipline and hard living.

By now 1943 was drawing to a close. It was during this period that I took part in an exercise which was connected with a plan for an invasion of Italy – another of my failed invasions, because I was not there for the real thing a few weeks later.

The exercise posted us into Alexandria in battle order; we spent the night in a transit camp, ready to set off the following morning. We were all in a big NAAFI hut and were very cold as the night set in. Just as we were trying to settle down a major came in, called us to order, and then told us we would be issued with pens and paper in order to write our wills and a letter to our nearest and dearest!

As you may imagine, this was not exactly a cheerful prospect. He tried to make light of it by saying that it was only a matter of form. But the army had to have a bit of paper on file 'just in case some of us are not quite on top of our form for the show tomorrow'. This was said with a jovial grin in the style customary at that time and widely practiced by Montgomery of referring to these little operations as though they were cricket matches which seemed appropriate enough if you are discussing them in the long bar at Shepherds Hotel in Cairo, but not so amusing when scrambling up the side of a heaving ship in the dark wondering what the morrow holds for you. At this point I began to wonder whether this was truly an exercise or the real thing, with the army kidding us – getting us to invade under false pretences, as it were.

So everybody sat down and tried to compose his last will and testament, and to write that letter. According to the major these would all be held in Cairo and only posted if we did not return from the exercise.

Just picture the scene – several hundred very depressed soldiers writing their wills, without so much as a currant bun to cheer them up. There was plenty of tea however – the army sailed through the war on a sea of tea – and there was also a large supply of mustard. So there we all were, gnawing the ends of our pencils, trying to think what to write in our last letter home and eating mustard sandwiches! I never did write it.

The next morning we went on board a ship off Alexandria with a lot of Indian troops and, after a rather rough 24-hour passage, we all came back again. I never found out what had happened to the invasion plan, but it was a debacle from beginning to end. We then had to get out of the bobbing landing craft, in darkness, up scrambling nets, and on to the ship. We were in full kit, the ship was rolling around and some men fell into the water, losing their grip on the nets. We did not see them again.

That was terrible enough, but my most vivid memory of the whole thing was the awful sanitation on board. Although I have described my experiences on the *Bergensfjord* and on the other ship that brought me to Egypt, I hope you do not think that I am obsessed with the state of nautical lavatories, but these were, if anything, worse than the last time.

Though the exact details escape me – mercifully – I do recall that there was a piece of equipment kept in the G 1098 stores known as a 'Plank, latrine other ranks, for the use of', or some such designation. About twelve feet long and about two feet wide, it had round holes bored every couple of feet. Placed horizontally over a trench of proper depth, it was, as designated, a perfectly serviceable latrine with seating accommodation for six or eight men.

These planks had been erected on the decks of the old cargo ship that was supposed to be taking us into battle. Buckets had been placed beneath the holes, as it was not possible, even for the army, to dig a trench on the deck of a ship. Unfortunately, the Indian troops were not used to the sitting style of latrine, and chose to stand on them. Used from a height, the buckets could not cope and the decks were, to put it mildly, in something of a mess. By next morning the majority of the men were ill from seasickness, or from the other conditions. It was just as well we were not to go into battle in such a state.

After another week or two in Cairo, we were ordered to embark at Alexandria again on to reasonably large vessels, this time without our motor cycles. We reckoned a long journey lay ahead of us but, of course, our destination was a military secret. Once again we worked out our rough course by the position of the sun and realised we were sailing west through the Mediterranean. We wondered if we were going to invade the south of France, and I harked back to my mad journey through France with Captain Ingham in his splendid old Lagonda. We anchored off Taranto, then continued our voyage. As day followed day, we kept our fingers crossed, hoping that we would pass Gibraltar. Sure enough we did, turning slightly north west to cross the Gulf of Cadiz, then sharp north beyond Cape St. Vincent.

At first nobody believed it, but gradually we became more and more certain. We were going home.

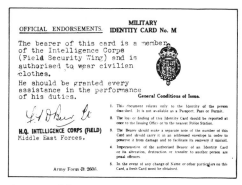

A very useful pass.

CHAPTER SEVEN

Back Home

A LTHOUGH WE did not know it at the time, we had sailed back to England as a part, albeit very small, of the preparation for what was to be the 'Second Front'. Everyone knew that sooner or later the allied forces would have to invade the mainland of Europe, so forcing the Germans to fight on two fronts. There was tremendous pressure for this from all the armchair generals and saloon bar pundits, especially those whose sympathies had long been with the Russians – since before the war and even at the time of the Stalin-Ribbentrop pact. But whatever had happened in the past was forgotten in the heat of the present. The Russians were our gallant allies. Why, even Winston Churchill the arch-Conservative had acknowledged the fact way back when Hitler had invaded Russia. Although he regarded Stalin and his commissars as 'completely outwitted bunglers', he knew that if they had Hitler as an enemy then they had to have us as friends. 'If Hitler invaded hell I would make at least a favourable reference to the devil in the House of Commons,' he wrote.

But all this grand strategy was unknown to us as we headed for home at the end of 1943. The only thing that mattered was that we would be back on familiar ground and reunited with our families for a little while. We docked in Glasgow on Friday, December 9th, 1943, and went ashore on the Saturday to travel by rail to London. At the station I was able to get away long enough to phone Rene in Upminster.

She was so completely flabbergasted at hearing my voice that the first thing she could think of was to ask whether I was phoning from Cairo! Oblivious to the fact that it had been impossible to phone abroad for the past four years.

I explained that I had arrived in Glasgow and hoped to be soon in Upminster. Her next comment was: 'Well, I'm sorry, but I've only got stew.' I said that stew was not the uppermost thing on my mind, and that I hoped to see her on Sunday. Which I did.

Having reported on the Saturday to Montgomery's 21st Army Group Headquarters at St. Paul's School, Hammersmith, we were given 10 days leave and, on the Sunday morning, I took the underground train to

Upminster. That day is recorded in my diary simply with a few exclamation marks . . .

Montgomery had selected St. Pauls, because it was the school he had attended. The 98th Special Field Security Section was absorbed into the Intelligence Corps presence at the HQ, and we kept ourselves busy ensuring that the plans for the invasion of Europe remained top secret. I would like to be able to tell you that I was really close to the heart of all that planning and intrigue, but the truth is that I had not much idea of what was going on, like 99 per cent of the personnel in Hammersmith.

What I did know was that there would be an invasion and, as my previous experience of invasions had not been pleasant, I was not looking forward to taking part in this one. The spring passed and towards the end of May our unit was re-assembled, we were issued with motor cycles once more, and sent down to range around the south and east coasts. For a few weeks we were based at Southend, which was ideal as far as I was concerned, because I could nip home on my motor bike whenever the opportunity presented itself. On one really memorable occasion I brought the whole unit with me and a procession of motor bikes turned up at our little flat in Springfield Court, Upminster. Rene did not turn a hair and managed to provide us with a very good Sunday tea! If you had to be in a war, we decided, this was the best way to do it.

Naturally it could not last. At the very end of May there was a clamp down on leave passes and security blanketed all the camps that had been set up along the south coast. No phone calls, no letters and no possibility of letting families know what was going on. I suspect that the very absence of contact told them all they wanted to know, for it was obvious that the invasion was about to begin. While I was not looking forward to it one little bit, I had resigned myself to crossing the Channel and doing my best, along with my comrades.

On the morning of June 2nd, or it may have been the 3rd as my memory is not clear on this, I was summoned to the CO's office and handed a letter and a travel warrant. The CO himself informed me that I had been posted to Preston. He also congratulated me on the contents of the letter. It was an immediate commision as a lieutenant and a transfer to the Royal Engineers.

I was absolutely amazed by this. I had no hint that such a move was even being considered. Having been in the army since October 1941, I had reached the exalted rank of corporal, been shunted around half the globe, done all sorts of odd jobs, none of which seemed to me to be the slightest use to anyone and now, on the eve of the greatest invasion in history, I was being sent up to Preston. Perhaps they were expecting heavy casualties and so were scraping the bottom of the barrel. I could think of nothing to say, but the CO evidently expected something from me, so I mumbled my thanks, threw him my smartest salute and cleared off.

1960: *Neuchwanstein Castle in Bavaria where I had learnt about 'commission'
'25 years earlier.*

1960: *Hotel Karwendelhof still looking the same as in 1935.*

1964: *25th Anniversary visit to Hotel Waldheim, Switzerland, still looking the same as in 1939.*

Above left – **1974:** *Town Hall, Sarnen; Paul Townend, erstwhile Travel Club rep and his wife Xenia (née Dansky), owners of the Hotel Waldheim.*

Above right – **1984:** *At home in Upminster.*

Below – **1984:** *Windmill villa, Vale do Lobo ('His').*

1984: *The partnership at Vivenda Irena near Silves ('Hers').*

1984: *Near Aramaco de Pera, the Algarve.*

1984: *Albufeira – the Algarve.*

1985: *Sagres (Cape St. Vincent) – the Algarve.*

1985: *Station Road, Upminster, much the same as 1935.*

An award from the Portuguese Government by their Ambassador in London.

1980: *Celebration of 40th Wedding Anniversary. Clockwise from left: Paul Chandler, Irene Chandler, Harry Chandler, Ursula Chandler, Michael Barratt, Dilys Barratt, Vladimir Reitz, Toni Reitz, Ken McCrea, Wynne Green, Tom Savage, Shirley Savage.*

1985: *Penthouse in Park Lane, not on top of the Cumberland, Marble Arch as hoped for 50 years ago, but at Hyde Park Corner with views over St. James's and Hyde Parks.*

1985: *Captain John Chartar, Commodore of the P & O fleet, with Harry and Rene Chandler on the bridge of the* Sea Princess *on her world cruise.*

1985: *The* Sea Princess *full speed ahead.*

1940: *Rene at the beginning of a fifty-year partnership.*

1944: *Springfield Court, the first Chandler home in Upminster. Harry, recently commissioned and on embarkation leave before departure to the Far East.*

1943: *007 on Secret Intelligence in Palestine.*

1943: *Still in Palestine.*

The letter confirmed what the CO had told me – the award of an immediate commission as a second lieutenant and instructions to purchase the necessary uniform and kit and to submit a requisition from the funds on my arrival in Preston. I think there was an allowance of something like £50, and I do remember taking myself to a military out-fitters in the West End and producing my precious letter. I walked out with a brand new uniform and a brand new single pip on each shoulder.

The only thing that puzzled me was why I had been transferred to the Engineers. Apart from my youthful experience with the Leclanche Cell, fitting up those doorbells in local shops, I am completely unsuited to any kind of technical work. I cannot to this day mend a fuse or put a screw in straight. I assumed that the Intelligence Corps required its officers to have some kind of specialist training and it was the bad luck of the draw that had put me on the train to Preston. But I counted my blessings, figuring that, since life as a corporal had not been too bad, life as a second lieutenant would be great. And a few days later, when the Normandy landings took place, I realised that I had missed yet another invasion and that many of those I counted as friends would not be coming back from France. I arrived in Preston with very mixed feelings.

Reporting to the commanding officer, I apologised for the mistake that had obviously been made, pointing out my total lack of qualifications for anything in the Engineering line and suggesting that he might care to send me back to the Intelligence Corps. He looked at me with the look of a man who has heard it all before – as, indeed, he had – and told me that on the following Monday I would be starting 'the short course' with other newcomers and it would be in my interest to make the best of it. That did not sound two bad, the way he put it, so I mentally prepared myself for a couple of weeks of lectures and demonstrations.

The 'short course' lasted three months. It consisted of physical train-ing, come rain or shine, every single morning at six, cross-country marches and hikes, classroom lectures and practical exercises in laying minefields and building Bailey bridges. I decided right away that I did not like the way the war was going for me.

Bailey bridges are easy things to cope with for anybody who has the slightest mechanical knowledge. Rather like meccano for grown-ups, once you get the hang of it. But I had no mechanical knowledge and there was absolutely no way I was going to get the hang of it.

Somehow I managed to survive the three months and, with the others, waited eagerly to find out where I was to be posted. When the details went up on the board I saw that, after a short leave, I was down to report back again to the very same camp.

'You're a lucky fellow, sir,' said one of the sergeants with a grin. 'You've been selected for the long course now. That's another nine months.'

I roared off into the CO's office, but he stopped my protests before I could get them out. 'Mr. Chandler, the army is like God and moves in mysterious ways. It also manages to perform wonders and if the long course turns you into an efficient Royal Engineer officer that will be a wonder indeed. But we do not argue with the army, just like we do not argue with God. Enjoy your leave and report back here as ordered.'

The long course turned out to be much like the short course – multiplied by three. The only good thing, I remember, was one of my fellow trainees, named George Skelton. Like me he had been an office junior, in his case with Pickfords, the travel agents. We were to spend part of the war years together and, after the war, he was instrumental in bringing Pickfords to the forefront of the travel business. He rose to become managing director of the company and was elected President of the Association of British Travel Agents in 1972. He did a tremendous amount for the travel trade, being a natural 'politician' and able in his quiet way to resolve doubts and disputes and keep things running smoothly. Sadly for all of us he died in 1978.

Our course was known as E10 and Skelton and I were given nicknames by the others – based on a couple of popular film stars of the time. He was 'Red' Skelton and I was 'Chick' Chandler, and the E10 group awarded us medals at the end of the course, as part of the celebrations! George got a medal for looking after me, and I got a medal for swimming the Ribble and for christening one of our lecturers 'Chinese Joe' because I could never understand a single word he said. He lectured on stress in bridges and on undistributed dead weight – uddw!

They also produced a sort of magazine to mark the end of the course, and I still have a copy lying around somewhere. Why did I swim the Ribble? Ah, that is an interesting tale, and the devilish Bailey bridge is involved.

Close to the end of 1944, the members of the course were split into small units with each unit being assigned the task of building a bridge. My unit – believe it or not they put me in charge – was told to build a bridge across the Ribble. We duly set about it, spending about 24 hours in the freezing cold up to our necks in the river. During this operation a boat broke loose and, as the river was in flood, it started heading downstream at a rapid rate. I reckoned I could make a good impression on the instructor if I recaptured the boat, so plunged in and swam after it. I did not manage to reach it, but at least I got myself back to the bank and was dragged out in a very sorry state. It made me a bit of a hero for that occasion and the instructor congratulated us all on our splendid bridge.

As the bombing had started up again in London, the flying bombs by now, Rene had written to tell me that she would come up to Preston for Christmas when we all had a little time off. It was a lovely reunion – I had booked us into an hotel in the town – but Rene could not believe the tales I was telling her of my military exploits. She certainly could not believe that I had the ability to build a bridge, so I took her out to the location the following day. We got to the river bank about three miles outside Preston and there was the bridge – gone! It had been washed away and was lying in the river itself. There was hell to pay when I reported back next day.

My time in Preston was the hardest that I have ever spent in my life, both physically and mentally. I cannot think it was anything other than a total mistake, but the army made thousands of mistakes at that time. I wonder sometimes how we managed to win the war at all, and can only suppose that the Germans simply made more mistakes than we did. The other people on my course were architects, surveyors and engineers in civilian life. My only qualification was that I spoke German, and so far in the war I had been posted to Egypt and sent on this totally inappropriate course. I hoped that my next move would make more sense. At the beginning of December I had been promoted to full lieutenant, and the first few months of 1945 saw me doing a variety of jobs in England. I had a spell on movement control in Liverpool, then went on a training course at Weavers Down, the Royal Engineers' training depot for railways. I thought the army was about to attempt to turn me into a train driver, but I found a lot of Cooks staff there, including Bob Smyrk who afterwards became managing director of Cooks. We were all trained as military forwarding officers.

This rather boring interlude was suddenly interrupted by exciting news which promised to transform my future. I was called for an interview at the War Office with 'Civil Affairs'. Germany was expected to surrender within the near future, and I was delighted to be told that I was to be promoted to staff captain and considered for a posting to Intelligence with the Allied Military Government of Germany.

Two weeks later, on May 8th, 1945, Germany surrendered. I held myself ready for an early posting to Germany to do a job more in keeping with whatever talents I had.

On May 20th, I received yet another of those familiar top secret and immediate movement orders. It instructed me to proceed to Avonmouth for embarkation on the *Monarch of Bermuda* – to sail for India on May 23rd.

The army had done it again.

The conditions on board were far different from those I had endured on my first voyage two years previously. In the first place I was travelling in the style that befitted an officer and a gentleman(!) and, in the second place, I had the company of George Skelton and some other good friends. I recall teaching George how to play bridge and the game became something of an obsession with us. We played for hour after hour, day after day, as the ship took us through the Mediterranean and the Suez Canal towards Bombay. We kept a careful account of the profit and loss and I know that I was owed several thousand pounds by the others. Needless to say, I never collected.

Although the war in Europe was finished, the Japanese were still battling on and we were prepared for all kinds of hardship and struggle when we reached the Far East. But first came an encounter with the Indian Army.

We arrived at Bombay in early June and were told that, next morning, an Indian Army colonel would be coming on board to address the assembled officers. The assumption was that it would be a real blood and thunder speech to raise our morale and tell us how to do and die against the filthy Jap. We were all prepared for that when the old chap toddled on board the following morning, a real 'pukkah sahib' type, all red braid and nose to match. His lecture lasted a couple of hours. The subject was 'the correct procedure for claiming pay and allowances in the Indian Army'.

We learned that the pay in the Indian Army was low by British standards, but was compensated for by the allowances system which would enable us to save a tidy little packet for our return home. To sum up the lecture, every single anna and rupee that was spent had to be accounted for by about ten forms, completed in meticulous detail. All these millions of forms went to Delhi where an army of Indian *babus* were employed as clerks. Each seemed to be either a 'failed MA' or a 'failed BA' according to the various visiting cards that later came into my possession.

We were first stationed in Bombay, where I occupied a small flat on the sea front. My first encounter with the workings of the Indian Army system came when I had to make a journey to Poona. First I had to obtain a travel warrant with all the necessary signatures, then I purchased at the railway station a first class ticket for myself to my destination. At a later date having collected and completed various other forms, I reclaimed my expenses first class return for myself, third class return for my bearer and also for the transportation of my horse. When all this was explained to me I said that I had no bearer or a horse but I was told not to argue and upset the system. So I got used to filling in the innumerable forms for my expenses in the time honoured fashion, and in the course of time the Clerks in Delhi would perform their complicated tasks and I would be credited with the approved amount.

The system was a recipe for complete chaos which, indeed, it turned out to be because a lot of the paperwork went astray. I suppose that in peacetime when there was time to spare the system worked fairly well, but in wartime it got out of hand and they just lost all count of the money. I had no idea then whether I had been paid too much or too little. By the time I got back to England and worked out that in fact I owed the Indian Army some money, I figured that if I kept my head down they would forget it. They did not however; in 1947 I received a demand by registered post. Because of the chaos, they had declared a moratorium on all debts, except for a nominal sum which, in my case, came to £27 and some odd shillings. I knew I owed them much more than that, so I agreed to pay, signed the form and sent it back. About six months later, I received a cheque for £27 and the odd shillings! I decided that the episode represented a most suitable end to my links with the Indian Army and that stage of my war.

But I must not digress.We spent some time in Bombay because it appeared we had once more arrived too late to take part in an invasion, this time of Burma by the sea from the south, but it seemed that events had overtaken us and Rangoon was captured from the north earlier than expected by General Slim and his 'forgotten army', aided by Chiang Kai-Shek and his National Chinese Army.

We then worked long hours on preparations for the invasion of Malaya, under the code-name Zipper, and I learnt that my own unit was to go ashore off Penang on D Day plus one, then thought to be the end of August.

At the end of July we were moved by train from Bombay to Madras, a journey which took about 48 hours and shortly after embarked on the *Minowai*. This was my sixth invasion attempt and with mixed feelings I wondered if this time I would actually see it through, having failed for one reason or another on the previous five occasions.

I was destined to fail once more for on August 6th the atom bomb was dropped on Hiroshima and the second on Nagasaki a few days later and the Japanese surrendered whilst we were at sea.

Before we arrived off Malaya we were informed that our landing at Penang would be unopposed. Thank the Lord that it was for we would never have survived the debacle which followed, another example of the Army cocking it up.

About a mile off shore Penang we came off the landing craft into about 3 feet of water in vehicles which were waterproofed up to 6 feet and set off for the beach. About half way we realised suddenly we had a problem, the water became several feet deeper and we had to abandon the vehicle, it seems nobody knew there was a deeper trench between us and the shore. Although the British had been running that part of the world for a century or so, an accurate chart of the coast had not been made. Or if it had, nobody had bothered to pass on that vital information to our Unit.

Can you imagine what would have happened if we had attempted that landing with the Japanese firing at us from the shore? It would have been mass slaughter, for we were almost literally sitting ducks. As it was, they ran out of the trees, down the beach and into the water in order to help us ashore. And, as for me, I could only conclude that I had been cast in the role of The Good Soldier Svejk of the British Army.

I was posted to Mountbatten's Singapore headquarters which had been established in the Cathay Building, about the only high rise building there at that time. If you have been to Singapore in recent years you will know that it is now a mass of skyscrapers, just like an Eastern version of New York. But then it was a low-level place, low in buildings and spirits after years of occupation.

Incidentally, it was during this stage of my career that I took advantage of the Army's ability to conjure up people with the most unlikely qualifications. I was given the task of getting open a large safe that had been used during the occupation by the Japanese, but left behind by them when they had vacated their headquarters in the Cathay Building, Singapore, now occupied by Mountbatten. The safe was pretty old and very formidable – a fine example of British craftsmanship, bulky and challenging and seemingly impregnable, and the keys nowhere to be found. Goodness knows what it had been used for before the Japanese took over, but according to local rumour it was now full of valuables. Gold and jewels and vast sums of money, claimed some of the locals.

I racked my brains over this challenge, wondering whether to get Army demolition experts in, but discarding that idea because of the damage they might do to the contents. Then my mind went back to those early days when the Army was teaching us new recruits how to ride motor cycles. If the Army could use professional speedway riders for that job, why couldn't it use a professional safe-cracker? Somewhere in Singapore there was bound to be somebody with the necessary qualifications. It was simply a matter of finding him.

After a consultation with one of the sergeants and a lot of telephone calls on his part – to fellow sergeants in other sections, to the Military Police and goodness knows who else – a smart looking soldier was marched into my office a couple of days later. I don't know where he had come from, or precisely what his qualifications were, and thought at the time it was probably best not to inquire too closely. For the same reason I never discovered if the two nondescript privates with him were a couple of his mates or a police escort!

I showed him the safe and saw the gleam in his eye as he examined it, rather as a connoisseur might examine a newly discovered Rembrandt. He left the office to collect what he called his 'little bag of tricks' and within a couple of hours the safe was opened!

Although there was no gold or jewels, the local gossip was right in one respect. The safe was crammed with money. But although its face value was astronomic, its real value was nil, for it was Japanese occupation currency and totally worthless except as a souvenir. I 'liberated' a few of the notes and have them to this day, and what fascinates me is that they seem to have been printed for use, not in Singapore, but in Australia and possibly even the USA! What confidence the Japanese must have possessed when that lot was run off.

These, and a lot of other memories, came flooding back to me at the beginning of 1985 when, along with Rene, I revisited Singapore for the first time in all those years. It has changed almost out of all recognition, but there were some familiar landmarks, including the notorious Changi Jail which, as you will discover, played an important part in my life story.

This return visit was possible because we were guests of P & O travelling on the magnificent *Sea Princess* as she completed a section of her round-the-world cruise. We sell a lot of P & O cruise berths, and this was the company's way of thanking us for all that business – several weeks of luxury at sea. I couldn't help comparing the situation to my early days, when all I wanted was a free third class ticket to Switzerland on the train in order to accompany my group of 15 fare-paying passengers! But even so things haven't changed much, for I was pressed into service as a courier to take a group of *Sea Princess* passengers on a three day visit from Shanghai to Peking – and had to do some fast reading in order to carry it off!

But enough of this disgression. Let me take you back to Singapore in those first few weeks after the war, and tell you how my military career progressed.

I was promoted to captain, attached to Mountbatten's staff, and appointed Military Forwarding Officer, Singapore. My first job was to go to Changi Jail and arrange passage back to Britain for all the prisoners. There were about 5,000 of them in Changi and other camps the Japanese had controlled since they occupied Singapore. For the first time I felt I was being given a job I could tackle with confidence, for in many ways it was just like being a holiday party organiser back in Upminster – the only difference was that my 'customers' were not paying me for their trip, and that I had certain powers to act on their behalf when it came to 'reserving' their transport. They were the kind of powers that would have come in useful in those pre-war days when I had to scramble for seats on the continental trains. It was ironic, really, that the wheel should have come full circle and that I should find myself acting as a travel agent for the army on the other side of the world!

The released prisoners of war were in a very bad way, ill and under-nourished and morale was very low. They had nothing apart from the rags they wore, so the first thing the army had to do was to treat them for sickness, feed them and issue uniforms and many soon began to improve.

But what raised morale more than anything else was watching the grand parade for the official surrender ceremony when hundreds of Japanese officers surrendered their swords to British officers of equivalent rank from the Supreme Allied Commander S. E. Asia Admiral Lord Mountbatten, down to the most junior officer.

This took place on September 12th 1945 on the Padang in front of the City Hall Singapore just three and a half years after the British surrender to the Japanese and I must admit that the sword I took from a Japanese officer, head bowed in abject humility, still remains one of my prize possessions. Rather than submit to this public humiliation, many senior officers had committed suicide.

Two other events happened on this day that remain clearly etched in my memory. We heard that General Tojo, Prime Minister and Commander-in-Chief of Japanese armed forces, had attempted to commit Hara-kiri whilst being arrested by Intelligence Corps officers, but had survived and was critically ill in hospital.

This resulted in long animated debates between those who resented scarce hospital facilities being devoted to saving the life of their arch enemy and wished to see him dead and buried as quickly as possible. The more vindictive among us argued that he must be preserved at all costs to stand the humiliation of a long drawn out trial as a war criminal. The latter view won the day and after more than two years imprisonment and several unsuccessful attempts at suicide he was hanged on December 23rd, 1948.

The third event of the memorable day was the embarkation of the first prisoners of war released from Changi Jail on the first ship to sail from Singapore since we landed the week before. We embarked about a thousand of them hardly able to believe that in a few weeks they would be back in the UK after many years of separation from their families.

The process of embarking the released prisoners for repatriation to the UK took several weeks and right at the beginning I decided to collect all their names and home addresses in the UK. There was no particular need for this, but I had a feeling that the list would prove useful at some future date – as it most certainly did.

After the prisoners had been sent home, I was given the task of organising transport for the officers and men being shipped home for demob. Once again, I collected all the names and addresses of the officers, and kept them carefully. I had the germ of an idea at the back of my mind, and it all stemmed from my efforts back in 1936 and 1937 to assemble a good mailing list for my holiday business. Here was the chance to collect several thousand names, by courtesy of the army. So I took it.

The local newspaper ran a big article with several pictures about our efforts, calling me 'the army's Carter Paterson'. I would like to think that if anybody in the army did the same job nowadays, he might be called 'the army's Harry Chandler', but I suppose that is being big-headed!

I had a great problem keeping some kind of control over the amount of baggage they were taking. When the Japanese had invaded, the local population had hidden all their valuables, but had brought them all out again in order to sell them to us. They did not want our occupation currency ('banana money' it was called), but wanted to exchange their goods for cigarettes, food and so on. There was an enormous amount of bartering going on, and a veritable mountain of luggage piling up on the quayside. The crisis came when my Commanding Officer came down to see me, bringing news that the captains of the ships were complaining about the amount of stuff being put on board. I could not impose a weight limit, because weighing it all would have taken far too much time and lead to all sorts of complications. So I issued an order that each man would only be allowed to take on board what he could personally carry.

They displayed a lot of ingenuity in managing to carry huge bags, boxes and bundles, staggering up the gangplanks as if they were on some bizarre assault course. On the whole, it seemed to work.

I settled fairly happily to my task of 'Carter Paterson' until, one morning, an unfamiliar officer walked into my little quayside office and asked if I was Captain Chandler. When I identified myself he said: 'I left your wife yesterday'!

I was sure there had been some mistake, and said so in no uncertain terms. 'Look here,' he replied, 'your name's Harry, isn't it? And your wife's name is Irene. But everybody calls here Rene. Right? Well, I left her yesterday in Rangoon.'

It was, unbelievably, quite true. And it had come about like this . . .

I have previously mentioned the WVS in Tel Aviv, where the ladies dished out tea to the troops and brought a touch of home, if not to the battlefield, at least to the 'theatre of operations'. Well, it had remained in my mind and, at about the time were were embarking from Avonmouth on the *Monarch of Bermuda* bound for India, I had spotted an official notification that volunteers were required. Volunteers were required for the WVS (Women's Voluntary Services) in India. They were evidently intended to do the same sort of morale boosting job for the troops in the Far East. On the voyage out I had discussed this with George Skelton, who said I was mad to think of suggesting to Rene that she should volunteer. It was bad enough to have me in the army, without getting her into uniform as well. I argued that we would not be going back to Britain for a very long time, if at all, and if there was the slightest possibility of getting Rene out there, too, it would not seem so bad. At least we could both be in the same hemisphere. I knew there was absolutely no chance of getting her posted deliberately to where I was going to be serving – that was totally against the regulations – but all sorts of things could happen by chance.

Anyway, I wrote to Rene and mentioned that volunteers were needed for the WVS in India. She had already volunteered to go into the forces, but had been turned down because hers was supposed to be a reserved occupation (they were making tanks at Fords in Dagenham). But she did volunteer for the WVS, was accepted and sent out to India about six months later. By that time, of course, I had left India for Malaya.

She reached Bombay, and then went on to Calcutta, knowing only that I was somewhere in South-East Asia Command. She was serving tea to the troops, arranging functions for them, dances and so on. The problem of morale was rooted in the troops reading about how the Americans were virtually occupying Britain, with the inference that the Yanks were bedding their wives and girlfriends. The German and Japanese propaganda broadcasts took every opportunity of spreading this story, so the WVS women were there to reassure the men and bring them a touch of home. They were the first white women most of the men had seen for a very long time, possibly for years, and when Rene travelled to India, she was in a group of about 20 women on board a ship with 3,000 troops. An RAF guard had to be mounted for them!

I now sat in my Singapore office digesting the officer's news. He had travelled with Rene on a plane from Calcutta to Rangoon; she had got off there, but he had continued the journey, having been asked by her to keep his eyes and ears open for a captain called Chandler who might or might not be in Singapore. That he had found me was sheer coincidence, but he was able to tell me that she was coming on down from Rangoon to Penang by sea in a few days' time. He even knew the name of the ship and, because I was in Movement Control, I was able to look up the records and confirm that this particular vessel had sailed from Rangoon for Penang the previous day.

I went in to my commanding officer, explaining what had happened. He did not believe a word of it. 'I haven't heard that any of these WVS women are being sent this far East,' he said. 'And in any case it's unheard of for a wife to be posted into the same operational area as her husband. It is strictly against the King's regulations.'

Patiently I explained that it was not a question of anyone being deliberately posted anywhere, but a matter of chance that was bringing my wife out East. I pointed out that I had been working particularly hard recently, and requested a few days leave. 'You're going up to Penang?' he asked, as he signed my leave permission. 'Too bloody right I am,' I replied, making for the door. He called me back and looked at me for a few moments. 'Captain Chandler, I have a feeling you are going to be disappointed. But I hope with all my heart you do find your wife. Something like this can do a great deal for morale. You know how damned sentimental soldiers can be. They love a happy ending.' Then he dismissed me and turned back to his paperwork.

The quickest way to get to Penang was by air, so I made straight for the airfield and cadged a lift on an RAF transport heading north. Once there, I went to the port commandant's office, using my best Military Forwarding Officer routine to get there. Once inside and past the orderly sergeant, I asked the commandant if he was expecting this particular ship. Not only was he expecting it, he told me, but it was in fact already off shore. He handed me his binoculars so I could identify it for myself. I told him that I thought my wife was on board with a WVS detachment and received immediate proof of my own CO's opinion that soliders can be 'damned sentimental'. The port commandant gave me the use of his launch and told me to get out to the ship without delay. 'Let me know how you get on,' he called, as the launch left its mooring. And he stood on the jetty watching us slice through the water towards the waiting vessel.

Once on board I was escorted into the presence of the officer commanding the troops on board. 'My name's Chandler, sir,' I told him. 'Military Forwarding Officer, Singapore. I believe you have my wife on board.'

'D'you mean young Rene?' he asked. 'Good Lord, yes, I've been playing liar dice with her all the way down from Rangoon.'

He put out a call for her over the ship's PA system while I stood wondering what 'liar dice' was. Within a few minutes we discovered that Rene was not on board; she had gone ashore to make inquiries about me! The senior officer and I raced into the radio room and put in a call to the port commandant. 'It's Chandler here,' I told him. 'My wife was on board, but she's on her way in right now. I must have passed her in your launch. For goodness sake find her and lock her in your office until I get back.'

Speeding back to the shore, I wondered if the port commandant would have better luck than I. He was waiting on the jetty, just where I had left him about half an hour previously. As I scrambled ashore he handed me the key to his office. 'Captain Chandler, make yourself at home,' he said with a huge grin. 'You've made my day, so I'm leaving early. My sergeant will be taking a prolonged NAAFI break, too, so you won't be disturbed for quite a while.'

I hurried into the administration block and gingerly unlocked the door of his office. Rene was perched on the edge of his desk, wearing her WVS uniform, looking out of the window at the harbour scene. She turned as I walked in.

'Hello, Harry,' she said. 'Come in. And close the door.'

Early that evening, back on board the troopship, the officer commanding the troops threw a party for us. During the course of what turned out to be a memorable evening, he took me to one side. 'Look here, old man,' he said. 'There's no reason at all why I shouldn't leave the ship here and make my way down to Singapore by air. If you have time left from your leave, you can travel down with your wife. You can use my cabin.' Rene and I thought the idea over for at least two seconds before accepting. Next morning the CO went ashore in the port commandant's launch, the two of them looking like the cats that had got the cream. I asked the CO to call on my own commanding office in Singapore and explain what had happened. 'Tell him that my morale is sky high, and the story does have a happy ending,' I said. 'He'll know what you mean.'

The CO's cabin was turned into a bridal suite with a mass of flowers that somebody had scrounged from shore. Our story flew round the ship and everybody seemed thoroughly delighted at the way things had turned out for the Chandlers. My commanding officer was absolutely right, for everybody was being 'damned sentimental'. I suppose that they all thought that if such a reunion could happen to me, it might just happen to them.

I do not know what kind of story the troopship CO told my boss down in Singapore, but it must have been a very good one. At the end of our 'second honeymoon cruise', as the ship eased herself towards the quay, a local army band was there to welcome us. And, right in the middle of the rousing marches, they got into top gear and gave a very spirited rendering of 'Here Comes the Bride'.

What a way to end the war!

CHAPTER EIGHT

War's End – and After

AS THINGS turned out, that triumphant arrival in Singapore was not the end of the war for us. After a while I was told that I was to be posted back home to await demobilisation. Now, as this was not due for at least another six or eight months, I had banked on spending more time in Singapore, if only to justify Rene's magnificent effort in getting out there to join me. But the army thought otherwise, as the army so often does.

We were not, of course, living in the same quarters, for under these particular and peculiar circumstances the army had no rule to go by. So it did what most large organisations do when faced with an unusual situation – ignored it in the hope that it would go away. It ignored that fact that Mrs Chandler of the WVS was married to Captain Chandler of the Intelligence Corps, it regarded us both as single officers and turned the requisite blind eye to whatever unofficial arrangements we cared to make. Although I felt honour bound to abide by all the rules and regulations, I saw no reason why they should not be bent as far as they could go, and reasoned that, anyway, what we did in our off-duty time was our own concern.

So for the first month of our happy reunion we spent the weekends together at, of all places, the YWCA in Singapore. After that with regulations gradually being relaxed she came to stay with me in my Mess.

My fellow officers and, indeed, everyone we came into contact with were well aware of the circumstances and many thought it amusing that a husband and wife were forced to behave from time to time like 'illicit lovers' – and I put that in quotation marks because I do not want to give a false impression!

Surprisingly enough, my Chinese houseboy remained unconvinced that I was behaving quite properly on those weekends when Rene came to stay. I had told him that my wife had managed to come all the way out from England to be with me, and he had smiled to indicate his pleasure at my good fortune and said: 'Yes, yes, sir. Good, sir. Good, sir.' When I introduced them, he smiled again and said: 'Yes, yes sir. Good, sir. Good, sir.' And after our weekend, when I told him how much Rene had appreciated his work and how much she looked forward to meeting him again, he just went into the same routine with a big grin, 'yessing' and 'gooding' for all he was worth. Then he scampered off into the kitchen to share this enormous joke with the rest of the staff. The captain had a girl friend and everybody pretended it was the captain's wife, and this was evidence of the very strange humour of the British, and the joke was even better when the captain pretended to be angry when nobody believed him.

So we spent several very happy months in Singapore in conditions rapidly returning to normal and made many friends amongst the local Chinese population who welcomed us back with open arms. I was kept busy in my duties as MFO embarking officers and men for shipment to the UK for demobilisation, both the British Army from Malaya and the Dutch from what is now Indonesia. Rene was busy also running several villas in the Tanglin Road as Hostels for the WVS, staffed by a motley crew of Japanese POWs, Indian troops, British other ranks and local Chinese civilians. Apart from that she was also organising the military post office in Singapore, but she became best known for the social occasions she was able to organise having about 50 ladies of the WVS under command as it were.

After this happy interlude the army decided I must return to England to finish off the remaining months of my service and although Rene was not yet due for demobilisation, by good fortune this event was brought forward by her pregnancy, and so it came about that, in July 1946, Rene and I sailed from Singapore together on the P & O cruise ship *Otranto*.

On our return to England, Rene went back to Upminster and eventually moved into our flat in Springfield Court. I was able to be with her, having been posted on attachment to the War Office. The army had to find something for me to do until my time ran out, so they first of all involved me in a high-level conference held in London for our military attachés who had been summoned from embassies throughout the world. I was concerned with the security side of the affair, and was fully conscious of the responsibility this involved, for the delegates were a powerful and very senior lot.

Lieutenant-General Simpson was in overall charge – he was chief or vice chief of the Imperial General Staff. Montgomery came along to lecture, but though I had great respect for him as the victor of Alamein and other encounters, I felt that he was too much of a showman. General Gerald Templar was also involved, being Chief of Military Intelligence.

The conference was due to begin on a Monday morning so, on the previous Saturday, I wheeled into the building to ensure that guards were properly posted and to check in particular that all doors and windows had been secured, all maps and documents put under lock and key, and that sort of thing. During my inspection I came into one room and found a rather scruffy civilian sitting there – a cleaner, I assumed. I gave him his marching orders very smartly, telling him he had no right to be where he was without a pass – which, of course, he did not have – and adding that if I saw him around the place after that he would be arrested. He apologised and left, and I felt that I had at least justified my existence that day.

On the Monday morning I was supervising the checking of credentials and identification at the main entrance when I spotted my 'civilian'. It was Templar himself, and he was making a beeline for me with a formidable look on his face!

He insisted on giving his papers to me for inspection and watched me check them. Then, as I saluted and handed them back, he learned forward with a smile. 'Captain, you are to be congratulated on the prompt action you took on Saturday,' he said. 'I am pleased to note that you are taking security seriously. Thank you.'

That little episode taught me something that has proved itself to be true on many occasions since. It is simply that, when a man has the brains and ability to hold down an important job, as Templar certainly had, he also has the confidence that enables him to keep both a sense of proportion and a sense of humour. I can think of scores of senior officers of my acquaintance who would have exploded at my behaviour on that Saturday, who would have pulled rank and blustered and stood on their dignity, because they had nothing else going for them. But not Templar. I must confess I often think along these lines when I listen to some of my colleagues in the holiday business. A few – too few – are 'Templars'. Some are all bluff and bluster, and very little solid achievement. But I must not digress, for I shall get around to my thoughts on the holiday business a little later on.

Let me stay for now with the army. Shortly after that conference, in October 1946, I recall, the army finally gave me work for which I was qualified – I was posted to Germany as a Political Intelligence Officer.

If you are familiar with the books about the Good Soldier Svejk by the Czech author Hasele, you will understand why there were times when I felt a great deal of sympathy for the character, indeed times when I felt I was living out the very role. I had been plucked out of the police force and enrolled into Military Intelligence because I spoke German and had visited the country. But apart from that spell as an unsuccessful code-breaker, the army had sent me to the Middle East, had tried to make an engineer out of me, and then had sent me to the Far East. Now, with just six months to go, the army was finally sending me to Germany. Better late than never.

I landed up in the town of Luneberg, a country town and capital of a small province which included Luneberg Heath, where the Allies had accepted the German surrender a year before. It was also where Goering had his vast estates and where he used to hunt. By then he was either dead or in jail, and the whole regime of which he had been a part had been consigned to the historical dustbin – or so we all hoped. Our task was to get Germany back on its feet again and, rather like helping a toddler take its first steps, propel the country in the right direction. To re-establish a free press and trades unions and a proper civilian administration – all the things to do with freedom and democracy that the war had been about.

The process of de-Nazifying our region was a difficult one, as anybody who had any kind of administrative experience would have had to have been a member of the Nazi Party in order to have gained that experience. The rules had been laid down back in Whitehall, but the civil servants who had drawn them up were clearly stronger on theory than on practice, and I would dearly have liked to have had them with us to see how they would have coped. In the first place, who was going to admit to having been a member of the party? To hear them tell it, every German had really been against the Nazis all along.

We finally selected the local newspaper editor to be mayor of the town – his main qualification being that the Nazis had closed down his newspapers because of his outspoken opinions. He turned out to be a good man, honest and honourable, and with his help we appointed other officials and got the province running again.

One of our tasks, as I mentioned, was to re-establish trades unions, and this was done with the help of veteran union leaders from Britain – men of the old school, not the kind of political jackals who seem to be snapping around the edges of the Labour Party nowadays. Volkswagen had a large factory in Luneberg and we introduced there the vertical trades union system – one union to represent all the workers, rather than a union for each skill or craft. As far as I am aware, this system is still working well throughout Germany. It is a pity that we did not put our own house in order at the same time, considering how well Germany has fared since the war.

Our unit included in its number a major whose name I mercifully forget. He was, I am sure, mentally ill, and besotted with his little portion of power. His main obsession was to weed out spies and, while there was no denying that spies were around to be weeded out, it was his methods that disturbed us.

At this time, thousands of refugees were flocking into the West from East Germany, and the Russians were sending their spies into this refugee flow. They were, in the main, pretty obvious – for one thing their fellow refugees were prompt to point them out – and we caught most of them and shipped them back. But the mad major reckoned that he could make himself a hero by catching more spies than anybody else, and one incident illustrates his obsession.

It was around two o'clock one morning when he woke me with the order to join him on a trip into the forest. 'We're taking some spies out, and we're going to get information from them. You'll see how I can do it, then you'll be able to do it too.'

I was not too keen on this. I did not like firing guns at people, and in fact had hardly heard a shot fired in anger throughout all my years in the army. However, I had no alternative but to join him and some others in a couple of jeeps along with two men who had just come over into the Western zone. One was middle-aged and the other was a lad of 19 or 20. The major was convinced they were spies. After driving us all into the forest, he stopped the jeeps and we all got out. Then he proceeded to question both the men who, having nothing to tell, kept repeating their denials. In the end the major, ranting and raving, said that he had had enough of them and was going to shoot them then and there. He told the soldiers to lash them to two trees and then blindfold them.

This was done and the major shouted: 'Shoot this one first.' The men fired four or five shots into the air, somebody cried out, pretending to be shot and the major quickly gagged the middle-aged man. Then he ran over to the young boy, stuck a pistol in his ribs and yelled: 'Well, do you want the same?' The boy was in utter terror, crying, shrieking and screaming that he knew nothing. The whole business was a sham and a shambles. After a while we took off their blindfolds and untied them from the trees, then took them back in the jeeps.

The incident sickened me, and I know it sickened the soldiers. That insane major, in my opinion, represented just the kind of madness we had been fighting against.

The other thing that constantly disturbed me was the contrast between our living conditions and those of the civilian population. They were all but starving. They had no proper shelter and we had to provide what food we could. I remember that people would go down to the railway station and huddle in the underground lavatories there, just to try and keep warm. That winter of 1946 was horrific, and I recall walking out on Christmas morning and seeing lots of children wandering aimlessly around in the snow and slush, wearing very thin and tattered clothes and looking simply awful. I gathered up a dozen or so of them and we brought them into our Mess and gave them food. It eased our consciences a little.

We, of course, were living as any occupying army lives – in the best possible conditions. We had private houses that had been turned over to our use, we had servants – German civilians who were only too pleased to be working for the army, because it meant they had food. I also had a car and was allowed to wear civilian clothes. As a Political Intelligence Officer I also had carte blanche to go where I liked. Now this is always a good thing in the army because nobody interferes with you, not even the ranking generals.

But I could not reconcile my living conditions with those of the German population at large. No matter what people told me about fortunes of war and the blame for it all lying with the Nazis, it was still a burden on my mind.

In December I determined to relieve my conscience of one small thing that had been nagging at me ever since 1939. I took leave and set out on

1944: *Singapore. Lieutenant George Skelton (later Chairman of ABTA) and Lieutenant Chandler cementing Anglo-Chinese relations.*

1944: *Singapore. The Military Forwarding Officer collects names and addresses of prisoners of war released from Changi jail for his future mailing list some of whom still survive as clients of The Travel Club.*

Above – **1941:** *Hermit Road, Canning Town (where the Chandler home had been) after the wreckage was cleared and the crater filled. Some Anderson shelters still standing.*

Left – **1944:** *Singapore. Homeward bound at last on SS* Otranto.

Below – **1947:** *The British first holidaymakers in Switzerland for eight years.*

1960: *The first charter flight into Albenga Airport, Italian Riviera.*

1935–1960: *25th Anniversary of first visit on the same tandem. Chandler is awarded the Freedom of Seefeld by the Mayor.*

a 48-hour journey to Sarnen in Switzerland. I was going to settle my bill at the Hotel Waldheim.

It was a harsh journey through devastated snow covered landscape in bitter cold with the unheated train stopping frequently to collect small amounts of fuel for the engine. The most distressing sight were the many thousands of refuges from the East living in goods wagons standing in railway sidings without heat and very little food or clothing. They were still there when I returned several days later. What a startling contrast immediately I crossed the frontier at Basle . . . Switzerland seemed to have remained exactly as it had been in 1939. Sarnen was the same. The Hotel Waldheim was the same, and so was the remarkable Frau Dansky. She greeted me like a returning hero, accepted my payment graciously and found the old account in her file, marking it 'paid in full' with a flourish.

She assumed that I would be re-starting my business as a holiday travel organiser and I assured her that when that time came I would be very pleased to bring my groups once more to her establishment. It was all done in a friendly yet formal way that went a long way to restoring my faith in the future, for the grim realities of Germany had depressed me greatly.

Back in Luneberg, I resumed my duties for a while, then took more leave and went home to Rene, hoping to be there for the birth of our baby. Unfortunately my leave expired before the great event – whether due to my faulty timing or Rene's, I am not sure – and I was back at Luneberg when I learned that we now had a son. We called him Peter.

I had hardly time to absorb this news and the fact of my new parental responsibilities, when I received an offer from the Foreign Office. It was time for my demobilisation, but they wanted me to continue my work in Luneberg as a civilian. I would be – a Political Intelligence Officer, Grade II, the same grade as my Staff Captain appointment in the Army, in the Control Commission for Germany. The salary would be £1000 per annum – the highest salary I had ever dreamed of up to that time – and I would also have the benefit of the house, living expenses, servants, and so on. I would, naturally, be able to take my wife and brand new son to Germany with me. The contract would be for seven years, at the end of which time I would either be offered a permanent position in the Foreign Office, or receive a year's salary as gratuity. They gave me a couple of weeks to think it over.

Back in Upminster I did a lot of thinking. We were living, the three of us, in that tiny flat in Springfield Court. It was the coldest winter for goodness knows how long, food was short, coal was rationed and the electricity was cut off for several hours each day. Conditions were worse than at any time during the war and I could not help but compare them with what would be waiting for us in Germany if I accepted the Foreign Office contract. I also knew that Rene was depressed after the birth of the baby, depressed by conditions generally, and I assumed there was no doubt in her mind as to what I should do. I assumed she wanted me to take the Foreign Office job – the soft option. After skirting around the issue for a few days, we finally managed to tackle it head on. I told Rene that the offer was a first class one and, in view of all the circumstances, it would probably be best to accept it.

In response to this she recalled our years before the war when I had struggled to get my little business going, and reminded me that she had done her share of the struggling and worrying too. 'You took the trouble to go back to Sarnen, Harry,' she reminded me. 'You are still interested in the holiday business. I think you should make some more inquiries here in London before you come to a decision. But it is your decision and you've got to make it for all of us.'

I thought about that 'all of us' as I waited to see the manager of our local bank. Being a father meant that the decision I made would affect not only Rene and me, but a child's future as well. I began to think about burdens once more, and the bank manager's attitude was less than encouraging. I wanted to know what arrangements the banks were making – or would be making – to supply money for people taking holidays abroad. He had absolutely no idea, made it clear he thought I was wasting his time, and referred me to his head office. So I went to his head office, and to one or two others in the City. Nobody, it seemed, was at all interested in financing foreign travel, and the people I spoke to thought I was a fool to be concerned with the subject.

Well, if the banks were not showing any interest, perhaps the railway would be more encouraging. I took myself off to Victoria Station, spoke to three or four different people, and finally go to see the man in charge of continental rail bookings. I asked if party tickets would again be available, as I had made much use of them before the war – for 15 paying passengers there had been a free place as well as a special rate – and I also asked about couchettes. Would these be available too? He promised to make inquiries and I received a letter from him about a week later. In theory, he said, party fares to Switzerland would be available within a year or thereabouts. The fare for London–Lucerne return would be £11.15s.8d. in second class and £8.12s.8d for third class for a party of minimum 15 persons. He had no news about couchettes, but pointed out that most of the railway bridges had been destroyed and the European rail network was in a terrible mess.

Discouraged, I started to compose my letter of acceptance to the Foreign Office, but as I sat in Upminster with my army greatcoat on to keep out the cold (the electricity was off yet again), something niggled at the back of my mind, telling me I had not tried hard enough to get information from the banks. Getting foreign currency was the most essential factor and, the more I thought about it, the more I realised that the ordinary banks could be of no help. I would have to go to the Bank of England itself.

That afternoon, wearing my best uniform with Sam Browne belt and buttons gleaming, I marched into the Bank of England and stated my business to a commissionaire who saluted smartly and directed me to the receptionist. I stated my business once again and, after a flurry of telephone calls, the commissionaire was called across to escort me to the office of a man named Johnson – a senior officer in the Exchange Control Department.

He was an elderly man, who had been with the Bank throughout the war. Offering me a seat, he asked what I had been doing for the last few years. He listened, apparently with genuine interest, to my account of my wartime experiences and we finally got around to the object of my visit: the availability of foreign currency for holiday trips overseas – in other words, the re-starting of the holiday business.

'It is difficult for me to be precise at present, Captain Chandler,' he began, 'And you must know that we in the Bank of England wish always to be precise. But I can tell you that certain regulations are to be drawn up concerning the provision of foreign currency. Indeed, we are drawing them up even now.'

'Is there anything else you can tell me?' I asked. After a moment, he nodded. 'Of course, people will resume the habit of taking holidays abroad, and of course there will be foreign currency available for them. As to our attitude towards the companies organising such holidays, I can assure you that, as far as the Bank of England is concerned, you will receive exactly the same treatment as, for example, Messrs. Thomas Cook.'

And that is what did it. That is what made up my mind for me. As I walked away along Threadneedle Street I decided I was back in the holiday business. Mr Johnson had given me the encouragement I needed, and that evening I wrote him a letter of thanks – on a battered old typewriter with the 'e' missing which I had carefully preserved since pre-war days.

I told Rene what my decision was and to my delight she thoroughly agreed. Only after I had made up my mind did she tell me that she dreaded the thought of going to live in Germany among the people I had told her about – the pathetic old folks and the scraggy, starving kids. 'I'd rather starve in England, Harry,' she declared. 'I couldn't be comfortable among all that sorrow over there.'

Many times over the years I have had good cause to bless the day I made that decision. If I had taken on that Foreign Office contract, I would probably have come back to England in 1953 having nothing but my one year's salary as gratuity, knowing nobody in the holiday business and being out of work. By the early 1950s all my competitors had got themselves established, and I would have had to fight for a place. I do not think I would have made it. My decision to come out of the army and restart the business was one of five or six major decisions that I have had to make during my life which, thank goodness, turned out to be right.

Perhaps more by luck than judgement. And I am also grateful that Rene has been there to advise and to guide and – yes, I'll admit it – to bully me into doing the right thing from time to time. But that is what marriage is all about.

All this happened at a time when most people in Britain were only too thankful to have survived the war and were not inclined to look too hard at the future. That chap at Victoria Station, for example, was happy that trains were managing to run on the southern region, let alone to the Continent. When I turned up talking about party tickets and couchettes he could just as easily have shown me the door, but I am always grateful that he took the trouble to make some inquiries on my behalf. The same goes for Mr Johnson at the Bank of England. In the aftermath of war he and his colleagues must have had some horrendous problems to tackle, and some serious matters on their minds. But he took the time to talk to me, and to encourage me. I suppose he could see some optimistic future, and in this respect he was a sort of guiding angel.

On this subject of optimism, I always think of Joseph Kennedy, who was American Ambassador in London at the outbreak of the war. He had declared that Britain was finished when France fell. When I had heard that, I could not believe it. Nobody here in Britain believed it. They thought he must be a Communist or a traitor or round the bend. As we know, he was proved wrong, but at that time any outsider taking a balanced look at Britain, uninfluenced by patriotism or emotion, could have said the same.

And even after the war had been won, it was hard to see a bright future. There was all the damage and devastation to put right at home. Industries were trying to restart, there were shortages and restrictions and extreme difficulties.

Under all those circumstances, that Foreign Office contract was extremely tempting. But my guardian angel was watching and I turned my back on it and got down to the job of starting up my holiday business again.

This leaflet was dropped over Changi Jail by the R.A.F. on August 28th, 1945.

On the reverse side instructions were given to the Japanese on the correct treatment of prisoners.

CHAPTER NINE

Starting Again

TOWARDS the end of February 1947 Rene and I set about restarting our travel business now with the responsibility of a family.

I well remembered that successful little holiday operation in Switzerland in 1939 with its £100 profit and wondered wistfully what this might have grown to in the intervening 8 years had we not lost this long important period entirely from our lives by the unseemly intervention of Hitler.

The most difficult task seemed to be to accustom oneself to the abrupt change from a disciplined to a civilian lifestyle. For eight years one had become accustomed to obeying orders, albeit reluctantly, your every move governed by other people down to the minutest details of what you wore, what you ate, when you slept, when you worked and where you went, all in accordance with some vast universal plan of which you knew very little. Suddenly this was completely changed, you could go where you liked, do what you liked, but there was no longer a universal provider and if you wanted to eat you had to earn the money by your own efforts. It was a difficult phsychological re-adjustment, and many men who had served years in the Forces found it impossible to adjust to this quite different mode of living.

At this difficult time I had nothing but my demob suit and about £100 gratuity to show for my years in the army, plus of course a nice letter from the War Office to say that 'the Army Council thanks you for your valuable services to your country at a time of grave national emergency and you are granted the honorary rank of Captain with permission to use it from the date of your release.

Another letter from the War Office invited me to volunteer for the Reserve of Officers Intelligence Corps and I signed up as a kind of insurance policy in case it started all over again.

I was now approaching my 34th birthday and realised my assets were very limited and it seemed we had lost eight years of our lives altogether. Then slowly I began to readjust to my new life and the new challenge. My mood changed and I began to think I was no longer the naive young-ster of pre-war days so greatly impressed by the discovery that you could earn money by commission instead of working at some dreary job. Hitler thankfully was dead, the war was ended and my knowledge and character vastly enriched by all the experiences of the past eight years. There had been many hardships and frustrations and some tragedies, but in general my war had been mostly a happy and rewarding experience in stark contrast with many others.

My slightly jaundiced view of the rewards I received for the previous eight years in the service of His Majesty was put into better perspective when I recollected a letter written by the Army Council in 1886 to my distinguished predecessor Mr Thomas Cook.

At the request of the Government, Mr Cook had organised in 1884 General Gordon's expedition to the Sudan including the transportation of about 20,000 troops, 100,000 tons of war material, hundreds of whale boats and thousands of tons of coal to fuel the steam ships. In the reverse direction they brought down vast quantities of cereals which they collected from the peasants in lieu of taxes and for the benefit of the British Treasury. This vast task, surely the biggest operation ever attempted by a Travel Agent, was carried out with extraordinary efficiency in extremely difficult circumstances. I had learnt of it from he book lent to me by a friend in Berkeley Street and it had made me a life long admirer of the company Mr. Cook and his son had founded.

The book had been lost in the bombing of my home in Canning Town, but I remembered General Gordon sent Mr Cook a note of thanks saying 'your agents have shown themselves most kind and obliging and have assisted us to the best of their ability. I hope that I may have again the pleasure of placing myself under your guidance', the kind of letter I like to receive myself to this very day.

The other letter Mr Cook received in thanks for this vast enterprise was from the Army Council and read 'I am directed by the Secretary of State for War to inform you that considering the difficulties of the navigation of the Nile, and the strain on local resources, he is of the opinion that great credit is due to you for the satisfactory way in which you performed your duty. I am Sir, your obedient servant'.

With that in mind I decided that my letter from the Army Council was quite adequate and I had been well rewarded what with the de-mob suit and the £100 for my somewhat meagre contribution to winning the war.

My sense of humour was restored to full strength, and with renewed energy and enthusiasm I threw myself into starting our small travel business. Rene and I devoted all our waking hours, and some of the night hours, solely to furthering our business to the total exclusion of all other interests, except our children. This hard but absorbing and rewarding lifestyle continued for many years until the business was firmly established.

My best asset was Rene who simply refused to be depressed by any of this and saw a future for us. As far as she was concerned we had the ability to make a go of it and our present circumstances were only temporary. She had that characteristic known as 'Northern grit' and, combined with my East End stubborness, it was enough to get us going again.

There were many practical problems to overcome. We had no telephone, and a telephone was essential if we were to do business. The Post Office said that we would have to wait months – or years – to be connected. Fortunately friends next door were on the phone, so we had an extension rigged up and existed for more than a year on this 'party' line. The lady next door was a schoolteacher and whenever she answered the phone and told people that she would 'put them through' to Mr Chandler, her voice and manner made callers believe she was a very superior office secretary! That impressed them no end. When she was out she switched the phone straight through, and Rene endeared herself to our telephone customers by telling them that they should not call in the evening at six or ten because she would be feeding the baby then.

And what calls we used to have. People rang up at all hours from early morning until late at night. They had all sorts of questions to ask about their holidays (this, by the way, was after we had launched our modest brochure) and it soon became clear that what most of them wanted was reassurance that they had made the right choice. There was one lady we nicknamed 'Mrs Wireless' because she used to chatter away so much. She, like so many other people, had been stuck at home all through the war and her first holiday abroad was a great adventure. Naturally she wanted to talk it over and over and make sure every little thing was going to be right.

Although I called it a prospectus, the 1947 effort was nothing more than a two page leaflet featuring a line drawing of the Hotel Waldheim in Sarnen, done for me by a printer in Upminster. But he was unable to print the leaflet, however, since – as with so many things at that time – there were shortages of paper and ink and other things. It seemed we would have no brochure after all. I managed to solve that problem by sending the whole thing over to Luneberg and getting my friend the mayor to print it for me on his newspaper machinery. I can thus claim to be the first British tour operator to have his brochure printed overseas but, unlike those huge companies who still do so, mine nowadays is a British product!

We sent it out to all the people on my precious mailing lists, the by now tattered pages I had collected from the Grove School before the war. Unfortunately many of them had been 'bombed out' or had moved for other reasons. Some had, sadly, been killed. We got very little response and this upset me greatly, not merely for the sake of my little business, but because so many of those lost names were friends of my childhood and my youth.

People have to take a lot on trust when they buy a holiday. They are paying out in advance – weeks and sometimes months in advance – for a product that is intangible. So it is important for the seller of holidays to have a core of customers who do have that trust in him. It is not easy to start from scratch, as we were having to do.

It was at this point that I reaped the benefit of another good decision: the one I had made in my little office in Singapore when those prisoners from Changi Jail were being 'processed' for home. I found the list of names and addresses and Rene ran off a letter from me on an old duplicator; I reminded them of who I was, the chap who had fixed up their trip back home, and hoped that they were now happily settled into family life. I also mentioned that I was organising two-week trips to Switzerland for ten guineas and that it would be just the thing for them and their wives and children. I painted a glowing picture of what Switzerland was like – plenty of food, shops full of goods, virtually pre-war conditions and a complete contrast to England at that time with its shortages, electricity cuts and hard times.

My ambition was to get 250 customers to go to Sarnen during that first summer, making a profit of £1 each. And in spite of all the difficulties, we managed to achieve this target.

But it was hard work, and I tried all sorts of ways to build up my precious mailing list. Acting on what I thought was an inspired hunch, I wrote to everybody named Chandler in the London telephone directory – there were a few hundred, as I recall. I simply said that, as my name was Chandler as well, perhaps they would like to buy a holiday from me. It worked after a fashion, and we got a few bookings that way. Indeed, I believe we still have some Chandlers travelling with us.

And, when I was actually accompanying my groups on the journey by ferry from Dover to Ostend or Newhaven to Dieppe, I worked another dodge. In those days the luggage was handed over at Victoria Station, loaded on to the ferries in a huge net, and left on the deck for the journey across the Channel. I used to go up there during the crossing and sit among the cases, copying down the names and addresses from the labels to add to my mailing list.

My first group left for Switzerland on May 15th, 1947, assembling for the journey at Victoria Station, just as they had done before the war. I met them wearing what I called my 'tour escort number one dress' – a very non-regulation army battledress and trousers – and went with them all the way. I had about thirty people in those parties. Most of them carrying a rubber cushion in accordance with my travel notes advising them to bring one of these useful articles in view of their 24 hour train journey on a wooden seat. But the journey was no longer smooth. France was still in chaos with all the bridges destroyed and in course of being replaced by temporary Bailey bridges. Oh, the memories that came flooding back when the train crossed its first Bailey bridge! Memories of Preston and those two courses that I had managed to survive somehow. Memories of the flooded Ribble and my Bailey effort being swept away. As we rattled on towards Basle I hoped the engineers who had built these bridges were better at it than I had been. We endured long delays, sometimes waiting for coal or wood to fire up the engine, and there was no water available on the train. By the time we got to Basle, many of my customers were in a state of collapse.

Then came the transformation. I had arranged in advance for the first class restaurant in Basle station to be reserved for my parties on those Sunday mornings, and for a full breakfast to be served. Eggs, bacon, cherry jam, fresh rolls and butter and all the Swiss trimmings – the kind of breakfast my clients had not seen in years. They fell on it like wolves and the waiters, who were full of admiration for the English, freely ladled out second and even third helpings. This raised everyone's spirits but, unfortunately, stomachs which had been living on a meagre diet for many years could not take the rich food, and there were always a few people in my groups who ended up being sick on the platform.

After this had happened once or twice, the porters complained about the mess on their nice clean Swiss station, so I agreed that I would pay a 'fine' of one franc for every person who was sick, thus satisfying honour and preserving good international relations all round!

In all, that summer I had about eight parties between May and September; accompanied them for two weeks and came back to Upminster for one week between trips. During that week I had to do office work and try to drum up more business. Rene concentrated all the time on answering the telephone, taking bookings and keeping the accounts up to date in addition of course to looking after the baby. It was hard, and left us little time to ourselves. But we threw ourselves into it because it was our own business, our own future.

My clients had little money to spare, so they were not inclined to purchase excursions once they had arrived at Sarnen. They walked everywhere because it was the cheapest thing to do, and I walked with them. Every party went to the top of the Pilatus, for example. This is a six or seven thousand foot mountain outside Lucerne which nobody ever dreams of walking these days. We not only went up Pilatus, but we also had the extra five miles to walk from where the hotel was in Sarnen. The hotel looks like something out of the *White Horse Inn*, standing in a beautiful spot on the edge of a lake and surrounded by mountains. But it is two miles from Sarnen itself. So I had a programme of walks and took out parties almost everyday.

Another problem we had, which remained with us for two or three years, was that the majority of my clients were women (most of the men had been overseas long enough). Because the hotel was isolated, it was vital to have a balanced group. As tour escort I was quite able to take them out for walks, or rowing on the lake, or swimming. But, in the evening, all I could do was to play the gramophone or organise card games, and this was when I would have liked some men to help me out.

So Rene and I devised a system which ensured that we got at least six men on each party: we accepted all bookings until a group was about half complete, and then refused more bookings unless they included men, so as to get the required number. This had an effect which we had not anticipated, because those people whom we had had to refuse (on the grounds that the group was complete for the week), assumed that the holiday must a good one if it was so popular and they made a point of booking earlier the next year! It is a lesson in psychology that the travel trade has yet to learn!

As time went by I was able to introduce excursions; I used the master ticket system which meant that clients paid in advance and were thus certain to take the trips. I earned commission from these, and also commission from shops in Lucerne. My technique in Lucerne was to tell my group, when we arrived, that they now had an opportunity to 'change their library books' – in those innocent days we had not heard of the phrase 'comfort stop' and would use all sorts of euphemisms for lavatory. Afterwards I would tell them about a shop which sold blouses and silks and nylon stockings and, of course, the women went wild for this. They used to almost literally tear the shop apart.

The first time this happened I went to the proprietor to apologise for the way my clients had behaved. He stood, beaming, among the scattered empty boxes and the jumble of clothing on the counters and the floor. 'Herr Chandler, let them behave as they will. As long as they buy, you just keep on bringing them. You will, of course, receive the customary ten percent on these sales.'

Until he said that I had, honestly, not realised that this was the custom – but I used to steer them towards the shop from then on. The other place they visited was a very up-market watch shop in Lucerne called 'Bucherers' where I taken the trouble to go in advance, explaining that I was the tour leader and wondering if the 'customary arrangement' would be made. My clients of course would pay only the prices shown in the window. It would be, I was assured. So my clients would buy from the one shop on the Sunday when we arrived, and from the other when we took our first excursion on the Monday morning. I figured that I should get them into the shops quickly before they spent their money elsewhere.

On that Monday excursion, I recall, we would take packed lunches and I would tell my group where they could go and buy a coffee to drink with their sandwiches. I do not suppose you will see that in Switzerland these days – 30 or 40 people eating sandwiches in a café and complaining about the cost of the coffee!

With the 1947 holiday season behind us, we took stock of our achievements, modest though they were, and decided that we ought to have some plan for the future. Rene was particularly keen on this, because it was no longer possible to drift from one year to the next, as I had been content to do before the war. The business would have to be expanded, but that expansion would have to be cautious if we were to retain control of it all. So we made some decisions that were to affect us for the whole of our lives.

I wanted to move to an office in London. In the first place, I had a deep-rooted desire to get away from my East End beginnings or, rather, from reminders of those times when I had had to struggle so hard to make ends meet. I also thought that a West End address was essential if my tour operating business was to amount to anything. As things turned out, it was impossible to find any office accommodation in London because so much had been destroyed in the bombing. We had to put up with our one roomed flat, although we did manage to get a telephone of our own in 1948 – what a breakthrough that was! But not moving to the West End turned out to be the right thing to do: it was an enormous advantage for the next 40 years to have our headquarters outside central London. It took other companies several years to realise the benefits of decentralisation. I suppose our failure to move from Upminster was a case of having the right decision forced upon us.

We also had to plan for expansion and, after a lot of late night talks and complicated calculations, we settled for a simple five year plan: deciding to add one centre each year. Starting with Sarnen in 1947, we would add Weggis on Lake Lucerne in 1948, then Pontetressa on Lake Lugano in 1949. In 1950, I decided, we would add Seefeld in Austria, and take advantage of the fact that that year would see a performance of the Oberammergau passion play – which I had visited in 1934. In 1951, if all went well, we would add Menton in the south of France. Along with this geographical growth went a plan for expansion in numbers – a modest rise to a target of 200 people to each of the centres. If the plan succeeded we would, in 1951, have a total of 1,000 passengers, each providing a profit of £5. An unimaginable income of £5,000 a year was our golden target.

Well, we more or less achieved it, at the expense of sacrificing every other interest we had except our business and our children. Oh yes, by the end of the five years it was 'children', for our second son, Paul had been born in 1949.

I have never worked so hard in all my life as I did during those vital five years. I managed – I shall never know how – to act as courier in both Sarnen and Weggis in 1948, but when 1949 came along I realised that, with Pontetressa also in the brochure, I would have to have some help. But could we afford to pay someone a wage?

I put an advertisement in *The Spectator*, seeking a young man for a job in Switzerland. The main requirements were fluent Italian and a good sense of humour. This produced John Boccanello, an Englishman born of an Italian father and an English mother. I told him frankly that he would not earn much money but would have a lot of fun as my representative, and he accepted without a moment's hesitation, taking my first group to Pontetressa in the early summer of 1949. He remained there for 20 years or, I should say, for 20 summers, for he returned to England each winter to take whatever work he could find. He stayed so long because he was treated like a king in that small village and had a most enjoyable life. The only drawback was that there was no prospect of promotion or any real future, so he eventually left to take up a post with Globus of Lugano, where he works to this day.

A stroke of luck came our way when, in 1950, I re-established contact with the Hotel Karwendelhof in Seefeld. The owners, Mr and Mrs Wilberger, remembered me from 1936 when I had passed through with Albert Goring on our bicycling holiday, and were sympathetic when I explained what problems I was facing in connection with the famous Oberammergau Passion Play. Because of the war, the play had not been performed since 1934 – its 300th anniversary – so the 1950 performances were heavily oversubscribed. There was enormous difficulty in acquiring tickets and I did not think that the little Travel Club of Upminster (as we now called ourselves) would stand a chance. Fortunately, Wilberger was a close friend of Anton Lang, who was playing the part of Christ, and I think Lang used his influence – and maybe a morsel of divine intervention – because our clients ended up doing rather better for their seats than even the mighty Thomas Cook.

All seemed to be going according to that plan of ours. The greatest challenge came in 1951, however, when I decided to offer my clients holidays in Menton. I was, in fact, offering a formula of sun, sea and sand instead of my usual lakes and mountains, and there was no way of telling how it would go. The paperwork involved was tremendous, for seats had to be reserved on the trains and rooms arranged at two hotels, as well as clients transferred across Paris between the Gare du Nord and the Gare du Lyon.

I also had the problem of predatory couriers working for other companies who thought nothing of roaming along the trains removing the reserved labels from my seats and installing their own clients. After putting up with this on a couple of trips, I got an engineer friend of mine to make me a solid steel 'T' key of the kind used by guards to lock carriage doors. I was thus able to get off the boat, nip along to the train and lock the doors to safeguard my seats. The temptation to lock my rivals in as punishment was quite overwhelming, but I resisted it!

Menton was a moderate success and by the end of 1951 we had achieved our goals both as far as the number of clients and the amount of profit were concerned. It was time for some more decisions but, as things turned out, the decisions more or less made themselves. Without hesitation both Rene and I came to the conclusion that staying small suited us, so we added no new destinations to our little brochure. All we now wished was to increase the number of our clients so as to increase our income.

We achieved this by improving the service we offered – reserved seats everywhere, baggage carried by porters at no extra charge, reserved meals on trains whenever possible, and small travel booklets giving information and tips about the five centres. In other words, we offered a first class service, albeit to a limited number of places. The only basic alteration to our arrangements was the improvement in rail travel which came with the introduction of first class seats and of couchettes and even some proper sleepers, although these civilized comforts were in short supply and you had to have good friends in order to get them.

The major change came in 1953 with the introduction of the turbo-prop Viscount aircraft. We immediately started to use the scheduled services of BEA, Swissair and Air France – night flights, of course, for they were cheaper. It was a major step to take, that transition from rail to air travel, but I was able to write in my brochure some lyrical accounts of travelling on a Viscount, describing how you could actually balance a halfpenny on the table in front of you as the aircraft sped through the skies at 300 miles an hour. Such simple explanations as this, I felt sure, convinced many people that flying was comfortable and safe. The age of mass holiday travel by air was dawning.

Naturally, my competitors were also aware of this change, and were adapting to it. At this time I regarded Cooks, the WTA, Lunn Poly and Global as my competitors, with Global likely to give me more to ponder on than any of the others. I had begun my own little business as a result of meeting those WTA (Workers' Travel Association) clients in Schwangau in 1935, and had modelled myself pretty much on WTA lines. Cooks were not in the same league, for they were the great giant of the holiday scene, with a tremendous history and a weighty reputation. They began, as you may know, as a result of one man's desire to spread the influence of the Temperance Movement (an irony to be savoured whenever today's travel people meet, for I fear we do have something of a reputation for bending the elbow!). But they specialised in arranging individual holidays for the very rich and came comparatively late to the business of organising holidays for the popular market. I often wonder what would have happened if Cooks had moved into that field much sooner. I doubt if many other tour operators would have had much of a chance to break their monopoly. But, then, the world is full of 'ifs', and there is no point in speculating on such things.

I was, as I mentioned, quite able to cope with Cooks, WTA and Lunn, but I recall Global starting up in Liverpool Street in 1950 and reckoned that they might give me cause for concern. This opinion was reinforced when I met a shrewd young chap named Sydney Perez who eventually ran the Global operation most successfully and is now a Director of Intersun.

It was, I think, in 1950 that someone came along to upset all my calculations – and those of other companies who were organising and selling holidays by train or by scheduled aircraft. His name was Vladimir Raitz, and the travel trade of today owes a greater debt to him than many of its members realise. For, in a single and most imaginative move, he brought air travel within the financial reach of many more holidaymakers and virtually created the low price package holiday by air.

While others were busy booking seats on regular air services, Raitz introduced the concept of a 'charter' flight. He would pay the airline a fixed sum for the use of the aircraft on a series of journeys to and from a holiday destination (in his case, Corsica), selling the seats himself at whatever price he chose. The airline was happy to receive a guaranteed sum and Raitz was able to sell an inclusive holiday in Corsica at much lower cost than the normal air fare alone. He had devised a method for undercutting any rival. It had now become cheaper to take a holiday abroad than in the UK. This was the basis on which the enormous holiday market of 10 million holidays per year was built. He chartered DC3 aircraft flying from London to Corsica seating 32 passengers, and provided the flights, accommodation in tents and full board for 2 weeks at an inclusive cost of £35.10s.

The principle should not have surprised any of us in the budding holiday business, for it was nothing more than the railways' 'party rate' ticket system applied to air travel.

For several years I had been badgering BEA, Swissair and Air France to let me have charter flights on such terms instead of the more expensive scheduled services that we had been using for years, but they always said there was a lack of aircraft. With the arrival of Raitz on the scene, I redoubled my efforts and, in February of 1956, I finally received a phone call from Max Keller, Swissair's general manager in London and a good friend of mine. He was offering me a charter flight between London and Basle on Saturday nights. The aircraft was a 44-seat Metropolitan and Keller was charging £660 for each flight.

Now we already had a holiday in our brochure based on scheduled flights on Saturday nights between London and Basle. To switch to a charter would provide massive savings, but we simply had no way of knowing if we could fill 44 seats a week. I asked Max to give me half an hour to think it over and then went into a huddle with Rene, discovering from her meticulous books that we had only booked an average of 10 people per week so far. 44 seemed quite out of the question. 'Should I ask Max to make it once a fortnight?' I asked. Rene shook her head. 'Do that and he'll withdraw the offer,' she said. 'It's got to be weekly or nothing.' We talked it over once again, drank a glass or two of wine to summon up the courage, then I rang Max back.

'You're on Max,' I told him. 'We'll take the entire plane for the whole summer. Every Saturday night, 44 seats.'

'I admire your decision Harry,' he boomed. 'You have more courage than Cooks.'

'What do you mean?' I said, fearing the answer.

'What I mean, friend Harry, is that this plane is only available to you because it was organised for Cooks and they have cancelled the whole series because they do not have sufficient bookings'. (This is now called "consolidation", a practice we have always strenuously resisted.)

Max went on, 'I have faith in you and I believe you can do this in Upminster. The best of luck.'

I put down the telephone, told Rene what Max had said, and we sat down to finish off the bottle.

Taking on Max Keller's Metropolitan proved to be another of those fortunate decisions. When I look back after all these years I have to admit that luck played a big part in things. Oh, we were able to make all sorts of calculated decisions about our little business, weighing up the facts and figures and knowing what the next move must be in this or that circumstance, but every now and again a big one like this came along and we had to take a deep breath and plunge in. Sometimes it went wrong, but thankfully those times were few and the repercussions not catastrophic. But when it went right it went gloriously, and in this case, most profitably, right.

In the first place, we had priced that particular holiday on the basis of a scheduled service air fare, which was now replaced by a charter flight at a considerable saving. We were, in the second place, able to fill nearly every one of those 44 seats on every flight by shaving the price a little (another good psychological move: telling people that the holiday would cost less than stated in the brochure brought in more bookings). We were also able to offer a combination of rail and air travel at the beginning and end of the season, thus filling up what the airlines call the 'empty legs' and our fourth great benefit was the way the numbers fitted in so neatly.

It speaks for itself, doesn't it? We had 44 seats on the aircraft, a 44-seater coach to carry out the transfer from Basle to Seefeld, and 88 beds in the Hotel Karwendelhof. With a combination like that, anything over a 90 percent load factor meant that we could not fail. We did not fail, and I decided then and there that charter flights were – to quote the late Lord Thomson – 'a licence to print money'. Twenty years later competition became so keen that those same charter flights led many tour operators to Carey Street.

During the course of the next two or three years we expanded slowly into other resort areas, including the Italian Lakes and the Italian Riviera, the Costa Brava and the Canary Islands, mainly because we could get good charter flight deals to these places. We were also forced to expand in numbers as the aircraft got bigger.

My next step forward came in 1960, by which time we had been chartering DC6 aeroplanes with 90 seats to Albenga, a little known airport on the Italian Riviera, as well as Air France Constellations to Basle, Nice and Perpignan. These were aircraft which were used on scheduled services across the Atlantic and we were able to offer 1st class seats at a small supplement – the first, and possibly the last, charter flight services to offer this facility. I then felt that the holidaymaking public would respond to the chance of flying on jet aircraft, which had then been recently introduced. At that time they were used only on high priced scheduled services, but chance – as so often – played a part in my plans.

At a formal lunch one day I found myself sitting next to Jack Bamford, the general manager in Britain of Air France. He mentioned that there was a possibility of a jet being available for charter, so I went around to his office immediately the lunch was over and we got down to business. By the end of the afternoon we were opening a bottle of champagne to celebrate what, I believe, was the first time a jet aircraft had been chartered for use on package holiday flights.

Shortly afterwards an Air France Caravelle was put at my disposal and I made good use of it, flying my clients to Basle from Heathrow early on Saturday mornings, bringing others back to Heathrow by lunchtime and then using the same plane to take others out and back in the afternoons – one Saturday to and from Perpignan, the next to and from Nice. It proved enormously popular.

But I'm running ahead of myself. This happened in 1960, by which time our lives had undergone a profound change. A change wrought by tragedy.

Dollars galore in a Singapore safe . . . See page 86

1962: *Our first venture afloat.* t.s.d.y. Iraine 1 *leaving St. Tropez harbour, able bodied seaman Chandler at the helm.*

1965: *The first press visit to the Algarve leaving the recently opened Faro Airport for the transfer to the Hotel Eva. The press were slightly put out to find we were not using luxurious Mercedes, but were soon mollified when they saw the crowds lining the route throwing flowers.*

1970: *The ABTA Convention in Rotterdam, the first one abroad. Vladimir Reitz, Horizon; Lionel Steinberg, Thomsons; Ray Colegate, Civil Aviation Authority; Tom Gullick, Clarksons; and Sidney Perez, Global, all pulling the strings.*

Above right – **February 1970:** *At No 10 by invitation of Prime Minister Harold Wilson to a party in honour of the Prime Minister of Yugoslavia.*

Right – **1975:** *Princess Margaret at ABTA Annual Ball at the Grosvenor Hotel.*

1975: *Limbering up on the tandem.*

CHAPTER TEN

Tragedy Forces a Change

W E HAVE come to a part of my story that is very hard to tell. Hard because of the memories it holds for me and for Rene. In order to tell it I have to dig around among those memories, and stir up the dust of time which has mercifully settled over them. And I have to try to express the kind of thoughts most of us keep to ourselves. I may not be very good at this, but please remember that for me that dust of memory is clouding my vision.

People who know us only superficially, perhaps because they, too, are in the travel business, tend to think of Rene and me as a pair of characters who have been around the holiday scene for more years than most. A pair who, on the face of it, seem a bit of an odd match, but who have managed to rub along together and make a success of their business. I have a tendency to get on my high horse and gallop around the columns of the travel trade press when given half a chance, and I know there are many people in my line of business who regard this with weary resignation. 'Old Harry's at it again,' they say, as I lay down the law on this or that. But that is the way I am – still that aggressive little East Ender who had ideas above his station and who was determined not to be put down. I know I am a nuisance to those who want a quiet life within our trade association, but I cannot change and I do not intend to.

But that is the public side of Harry Chandler and, though the private side has all those characteristics too, there is more in my makeup than superfiical acquaintances will ever discover. The same is true of Rene. She had it tough when she was a youngster, just like I did. And she has known tough times since being married to me. Again, those superficial judgements of us cannot take any of that past into account. The travel world – and other acquaintances – see only the Chandlers of today. A writer once described us in a woman's magazine article as 'living in a state of armed truce' – or something like that. He was taken in by our continual banter and judged us only in terms of our present day material possessions. He could not see the depths of our relationship, the strength of a marriage that has lasted as long as ours. To outsiders we may seem an odd pair, but we suit each other very well all the same.

This might be as good a time as any for me to try and express something of the love I have for Rene and to acknowledge the debt I owe her. Being a typical Englishman, it is not easy for me, and I shall have to hide behind the clichés that people use on such occasions. But cliché or not, Rene has been a tower of strength during our marriage and a steadying influence whenever I looked like galloping off out of control. Without her presence during these years immediately after the war, I do not think I would have had the perseverance to build up my business. If she had not kept a close eye on the detailed routine work in our tiny flat-cum-office, I would not have been able to flash around taking the plunge into this or that direction.

And Rene is still that steadying influence, providing the hand that every man needs, pushing me on when I need a push, and reining me in when I look like getting out of control. I am the one who gets all the publicity within the travel trade, the one who is interviewed by the media, and Rene would be less than human if she did not resent this just a little bit from time to time. But though others may not acknowledge it, I never lose sight of the fact that the Chandlers are a true partnership, and we need each other very much.

I do not think I could put it better than the journalist who once described me as the bright kite, soaring and swooping through the air and attracting all the attention. 'But no kite flies free,' he wrote. 'And Rene Chandler's skill with the guide strings is as important as Harry's displays. She stops him soaring off into the stratosphere and keeps him from crashing into the ground.'

Let me tell you what happened to us Chandlers in the late 1950s, when our prospects were improving and we could see that, with a lot of hard work and a little luck we might soon be running a profitable business. We decided to pass on some of this benefit to our sons, Peter and Paul by providing them with a public school education. They were going to a very good local school but, after talking it over between ourselves and with their head teacher, we took the plunge and enrolled them in Felsted School, the plan being that they should both start there at the age of eight or nine. I took out an insurance policy to cover the fees – it was £300 a year then, I recall, which would be about £3,000 a year now – and, when he was nine years old, Peter duly started as a boarder there.

Something like three years later – in the summer of 1959 – we were all together as a family, with Peter home for the school holidays and young Paul looking forward to going with him to Felsted at the beginning of the autumn term. For Paul it would be 'big school' with his big brother. For Peter, the opportunity of giving a helping hand to a very special new boy at Felsted. So there we were, with the summer holidays coming to an end and all our prospects bright. Then Peter suffered an attack of headaches and vomiting one night. The next day we called in our local GP and he suggested strongly that Peter should be thoroughly examined at the local hospital.

During the previous Easter we had gone skiing in Austria, but Peter had not enjoyed this as he had complained of headaches and sickness. We had then assumed that it was something to do with the altitude, and this assumption had been strengthened when the symptoms ceased on his return to England. Now it had happened again.

The extraordinary thing was that Peter's attack had come the very day before the two boys were supposed to go to Felsted School; we were actually on our way there when we called into the hospital for what we thought would be a short examination. In the event, the specialist suggested that we should take Paul on to school and return for Peter when we had done so. It seemed a bit hard on little Paul, to be all alone on his very first day, but we did as the specialist suggested and called back at Brentwood Hospital on that Friday afternoon.

The surgeon had a kind and gentle manner, but was firm in his opinion that Peter should undergo an operation – an exploratory operation, he called it – as soon as possible. He suggested Monday morning. 'Take your son home now,' he said. 'Enjoy the weekend. Do whatever you usually do. And bring Peter here on Monday.'

When something like this happens, should the surgeon be reassuring or realistic? Did we want him to spell out exactly what was wrong with Peter? Or did we want him to tell us everything would turn out fine? I cannot say what I would want to be told if such circumstances arose again in my life. All I know is that we drove home in silence and tried to make the most of that weekend. As far as Peter was concerned, he was going back for another check-up and some minor surgery, although a youngster not yet 12 cannot be expected to worry himself too much over that. To him, illnesses were a nuisance and something to be cured with medicine and pills. Kid's stuff.

So we took ourselves off to Southend on the Saturday, and went on to Kursall. We toured the sideshows and went on the rides and the roundabouts and had a terrific time. By Monday morning were half-inclined to think it was just another juvenile illness that would be sorted out in no time, so we delivered Peter back to the hospital and went home to wait.

'Ring at midday for a progress report,' they had said. This we did, and were told that Peter was still in surgery. 'Call in this evening,' they said.

Peter was heavily bandaged about the head and, though he looked terrible, he was quite conscious and articulate. He told us that one of the nurses had explained everything to him, how the surgeon had had to cut a little hole in his head in order to see what was wrong and had found something called a tumour. Peter was not sure what a tumour was, but the nurse had told him that the surgeon was hoping to take it away. Unfortunately it was in an awkward place.

You could wrap all that up in the most fancy medical jargon, but the facts would remain the same. An operation was vital if Peter's life was to be saved. But that very operation might kill him. These days they call it Catch-22.

We went in to see him every day for the next three days while the surgeon and his team agonized over their decision. As far as we could tell, Peter was bearing up remarkably well and we hoped this was a good sign. Youth and strength were on his side.

In the small hours of Friday morning, at around two or three o'clock, we were woken by the front doorbell. Rene and I hurried down to find out who on earth it could be. On the step were two police constables. They had come to inform us that Peter was dead.

We were told, later, that there had been no hope. An operation had been impossible. Some time afterwards, one of our friends who was a doctor said that it was a mercy that Peter had not recovered. It was very hard for Rene and I to accept this, but he explained that the boy would have been completely helpless. As the years have passed I have come to appreciate the sense of what he said, but that is, of course, because the dust of time has settled over that memory.

No words can describe the shock that came over us at Peter's death. I had had members of my family killed in the war, but that was when death came from the skies and claimed many victims. This was totally and terribly different. Both Rene and I were in a distraught state, but we knew that we had to break the news to Paul. I thought we should bring him home from Felsted School which he had joined as a boarder, but Rene and the doctors emphatically disagreed. So did the headmaster. Once again I could not see the sense of this at the time, but leaving him at school was the right course to take. We went up to see him and break the news, taking him away from the school for a day.

After we had returned him to Felsted and said our farewells, Rene and I drove back to Upminster. We knew that our lives could never be the same again.

Until that time, we had had no interests other than our business and our family. Both Rene and I had worked in the office for up to 16 hours every day and spent the rest of the time either playing with the boys or sleeping. We were now forced to re-assess our lives; we had to break out of this pattern and do something quite different. We thought of various things. I wondered whether I could learn to fly, and actually went down to Southend airport to make some inquiries. For one reason or another I was put off that idea, so Rene and I then embarked on a series of trips around the countryside. Then I had a brainwave. I decided we should have a boat.

Now, apart from travelling on troopships during the war I knew absolutely nothing about the sea and was totally ignorant about boats. I was such an ignoramus, in fact, that when I got the idea all I could think of doing was go to the local papershop and buy a yachting magazine, hoping to find a boat in the 'for sale' column. There were hundreds of them, and the more I read the advertisements, the more confused I became. However, I saw one being offered by a man who called himself a yacht agent and whose address was not too far away. He gave an out-of-hours telephone number, so I dialled it then and there on that Saturday evening. As I waited for him to answer I scanned the 'for sale' pages and saw that he had a lot of boats on offer, all illustrated with nice little photographs. I decided that buying a boat was an easy thing to do and was in a very enthusiastic mood when he picked up the reciever.

We exchanged a few words and then got down to business. I described the particular boat I wanted – a 45 foot cruiser that would sleep half a dozen people. He seemed to think that something less ambitious would suit a beginner, but I insisted it was just what I wanted. 'I'll come and see you tomorrow,' I said. 'You can show me over this boat and I'll look at some of these others you have.'

As tactfully as possible he explained that as a yacht agent he represented the owners of boats scattered all over the country. The vessels were not, as I had imagined, all tied up in one place, like a used car lot. Having got that sorted out, he pointed me in the right direction and, over the course of the next two or three weeks, I saw several craft. Although I did not buy the particular 45 footer that had first caught my eye, I did buy one very much like it three weeks later – a 45 foot cruiser with twin screw diesel engines, moored in Poole Harbour.

Its owner was a retired naval captain. At least, he claimed to be a retired naval captain, but I have my doubts about that in view of what happened after I had paid him the £5,000 asking price. He had on board a tiny wizened old man who looked after it for him and this old fellow wanted to know when I would be taking delivery, as he would have to find himself somewhere else to live. As it was by now February he doubtless assumed I would be coming back in the spring to claim ownership. But having paid for the boat I was not in the mood to wait, and I told him I would be taking it there and then – sailing it up the Channel, round into the North Sea and across the Thames Estuary to Burnham-on-Crouch.

He looked at me as if I was insane and, with hindsight, I agree with his diagnosis. I was armed only with a motorist's atlas of Britain and planned to navigate from that. I had no idea of the 'rule of the road' at sea, but when the old man pointed all this out, I just told him not to worry as it was a lovely day, with the sun shining and the sea calm. He then asked if I had heard the shipping forecast for the next couple of days, and it dawned on me that the journey by sea would take longer than the journey down by road had done.

Rene had driven me down, but I was not going to be alone on my voyage because I had three friends with me, neighbours from around Upminster. They knew nothing about boats either, but we reckoned that boats would be as easy to handle as cars and it was merely a matter of gaining experience. Rene was going to drive back to Upminster and then go, with their wives, to meet us at Burnham-on-Crouch. The way we had it planned, it would be as easy as falling off a log. Were we such innocents!

When he realised that he could not persuade us to change our plans, the old man took us all out for a ride around Poole Harbour, to give us an idea of the controls and the handling of the cruiser. We then unpacked all the food we had brought and stowed it on board. As we were about to leave the old man called out from the quayside, but I could not make out what he was saying. One of the others heard him, however, and reported that he had said something about a five gallon drum of oil that had been stowed in one of the lockers. 'He says we might need it before the trip is over,' said my chum. At the time I thought nothing of this.

Off we set, four men in a boat, enjoying the sunshine and thinking that this was certainly the life. Twenty minutes or so later we ran into thick sea mist, and one of the engines started to overheat.

Fortunately one of my 'crew', Roy Middleton, was a garage owner and knew plenty about engines. He prised open the small hatch and went down to take a closer look, calling up within a few seconds that the faulty engine was running dry as all its lubricating oil had gone. 'That's no problem,' says I, 'for we have a spare five gallon drum in one of the lockers. That's a bit of luck.' He took the drum and poured the oil into the engine. To our amazement it soaked up every drop, but I assumed that this was because the old man had simply forgotten to put oil in. We crept forward carefully through the mist, but within half an hour that same engine was overheating again. Down went Roy into the inspection hatch, reporting back that the engine was once again bone dry and the entire five gallons of oil was swilling about in the bilges. I would like to repeat in detail the language he used to make this report, and our language in describing the 'ex-naval captain' and his lunatic Ben Gunn of a mechanic, but this book might fall into the hands of susceptible young people of the more sensitive kind, such as travel agency counter clerks, to whom such words are, of course, quite unknown!

There was nothing for it but to shut off the wonky engine and use the one remaining. It cut down our manoeuverability and made steering generally difficult, but we had no choice. The mist showed no signs of clearing, but I had fallen easily into the role of captain and posted one of my friends to stand by the bell and ring it every half minute, keeping his ears open for any other ships or hazards. The sea started to get rough and we began to feel queasy. The voyage was not working out at all as planned and my atlas was of little help as we hung on to whatever we could grab with the ship tossing around in the gloom like a frenzied cork.

Suddenly we heard a bell ringing. It confirmed my vague suspicion that by now we were somewhere near the Needles, for it was the bell on the lighthouse. I said as much, and one of my friends said 'Don't you mean light ship?'

'No,' I replied, 'lighthouse'.

'I'm sure it's a light ship.'

'Lighthouse.'

'Are you sure?'

'Of course I'm sure. It's marked on my atlas.'

'I think there's a lighthouse and a light ship' – came the contribution from one of the others that we could have done without.

'What difference does it make?'

'What difference? What difference? Only the difference between drowning in deep water or smashing on the rocks, that's all.'

'I still think it's the lighthouse.'

'Are you sure it isn't the light ship?'

We could have gone on with this *Monty Phython* dialogue for a couple of hours as we drifted nearer and nearer to the sound of the bell. We were all talking at once and, if the ship had not been bobbing about so much, we would probably have been flapping our arms and running around in every decreasing circles.

'We just can't go on like this,' I said, trying to sound commanding. 'Can anyone tell where the sound is coming from?' I should not have asked. There was a chorus of 'Over there', 'no, over that way,' 'left', 'right'.

'Don't you mean port?'

'Where's port? Is that the same as right?'

'No I think it's the same as left.'

'What difference does it make?'

'What difference? What difference? Only the difference between life and death, mate. That's all.'

Suddenly there was a scream from one of my companions. 'Rocks!' he yelled. 'Bloody rocks. There.'

A few yards ahead were enormous breakers, so I instinctively threw the wheel hard over and ran the engine at maximum speed. We slithered away from the rocks and I headed out into the Channel. I had had enough of this brave sailor lark to last me a lifetime. We eventually put down the anchor in about forty feet of water in Bournemouth Bay and lay out on the deck as the boat heaved and tossed through the night. We were all sick as dogs and I resolved that, when dawn broke, I would find the nearest harbour and sell the damned boat. So far I had escaped death by inches, and I did not fancy risking it again. So the night passed by and as dawn broke the fog cleared so we could see pale stars. The sea calmed and the sun rose. It was a glorious morning and we all felt much better and set off in high spirits to continue our journey. I forgot about selling the boat and decided sailing suited me. It was just a matter of using the proper maps instead of an old road atlas and working out which side of the buoys you had to go. We trundled along on one engine, heading for Ramsgate. There we tied up to the quay and scoured the shops for some big washers to plug all the leaks in the engine. Roy made temporary repairs, saying he had not enjoyed himself so much for ages and thought boat engines were a real challenge and a lot more fun than cars. I suppose we were like kids playing with a new toy, but it occupied us so totally that we quite forgot about our original timetable. And about the wives waiting for us. I did not even bother to ring Rene from Ramsgate to tell her what had happened and that we would be a couple of days longer than planned.

Because of this, the wives of the other three got into a real panic and telephoned Rene, expecting that she would have heard something. She had not, of course, but reassured them that we would be all right. She was quite calm because, unlike the others, she had not read in the papers about the havoc caused to shipping by the gales in the Channel. We ourselves had not known it at the time either, but we had been in a Force Eight as we bobbed about just off the Needles. Talk about ignorance being bliss!

Eventually we reached Burnham. I telephoned Rene, and she and the other wives came down to meet us. Her first words on seeing me was that I had never looked so well in my life and sailing obviously suited me. I was, she said, as fit as a fiddle. Of course, I had eaten very little on the trip and had moreover, lost about half a stone through seasickness. I was burned by sun and wind and I suppose this made me look fit. Anyway, Rene decided that the nautical life suited me.

Well, that was my introduction to boating, and I have had a lot of fun and some mild adventures ever since. The main thing at that time, however, was that it helped to stop our minds brooding. It could not wipe away the memories and the worries entirely, but it helped.

After a little while, I became more confident and took Rene along to Burnham in order to get her involved as well. On our first weekend, I fancied myself as the skipper, so I put on my white trousers and little peaked cap and drove out on the river. I was not going to risk anything as ambitious as actually going to sea!

We were bowling along merrily, with Rene relaxing on deck sun-bathing and both of us deciding this was a most pleasant way of passing time. Then, I remember, Rene reached over to get something from her handbag and, as she did so, a five pound note fluttered off and blew over the side into the water. We watched it soak and sink. Though I did not realise it at the time, that little incident was symbolic of owning a boat. Somebody once said that yachting was like standing under a cold shower tearing up £5 notes – and I know very well what he meant. A boat is enormously expensive, and quite out of all proportion to other expenses, but we have had a tremendous lot of fun and satisfaction out of boats.

Let me tell you a little bit more about that first boat. Of course, I realised that I had been sold a pup because that one engine was full of leaks, and Roy said the engines would have to come out completely if the repairs were to be carried out properly. He did just that; after all, they were over 25 years old. That first vessel of ours was a good old teak boat, but we always had trouble with it. We ventured further afield as our confidence grew – to Holland one year. The next year we went across to

Holland again, intending to go into the Baltic, but we never made it because that wretched engine packed up again.

The following year we decided to take it into the Mediterranean, just Rene and I, Paul, another chap and an au pair girl we had working for us at the time. The plan was to cross the Channel, go up the Seine to Paris, then down by rivers and canals to Sete, near Marseilles. We knew that we would have to keep coming back during the trip because it would take a long time – there are 300 locks on the canal between Paris and Sete – and we had work to do in Upminster.

All went well at first. We had a pleasant week's holiday and flew back with Paul from Paris, leaving the other two to start off down the canals. It took them a couple of weeks to get to Dijon, which is where they were when we flew back. We stayed on board for another week, going down the canal, and then flying back home again. For six or seven weeks the boat travelled gently down through the wine country, with Rene and I flying out to join it every now and again.

I cannot recall exactly how it happened, but for some reason or other the young chap and the au pair girl had to come back to England and I got two other young fellows to take the boat on down to Sete, and then to Marseilles. Rene and I did not get on very well with them. One was a dental student who had failed his examinations about six times and, at 27 or 28, was getting too old to be a student. After a week, a row broke out between us.

We had come into a little harbour – Frejus, I think – with me at the wheel, and had to drop our anchor among a lot of fishing boats which had long lines out. Next morning we started the engine and found we were held fast because a line had got tangled around the screw. It is an easy thing to do when fishing boats are around. I pointed this out to the dental student, expecting that he would go overboard and clear the obstruction. But he would not do it, he said, 'not for a thousand pounds'. Whether he was worried about getting his hair wet or whatever, his attitude was really annoying me, because he was so much younger than me and should have had no hesitation about going over. So I decided to show him how to do it. By this time we had a lot of French people lined up on the quayside, all anxious to see us make fools of ourselves. To show that I did not give a hoot for them, I dived overboard in the approved fashion with a knife in my teeth. I was able to cut the line free very quickly, and as soon as it floated to the surface this damn fool of a fellow started the engine and moved off across the harbour.

I yelled at him to hang on, and he yelled back at me to go ashore. What he wanted me to do was walk along the jetty so he could pick me up at the end, but I did not realise this and was so furious that I just swam right after him. At this point Rene came on deck, saw what was happening and told him to cut the engine immediately. He did as he was told, I got on board and had a tremendous row, telling him to clear off in no uncertain terms.

Off he went and we eventually continued the journey by ourselves – I, Rene, Paul, who was then about ten years old, and the au pair girl who had rejoined us and spent most of her time sitting in the sun. We all had a marvellous time, going along to San Remo and Alassio and eventually to Menton where we decided to leave the boat. And there it stayed for ten years. As we were running a charter flight to Nice, it was quite easy to take a week there fairly often. Then Nice fell out of fashion, so for quite a long time we neglected our boat. By then it needed a lot of repairs, so I made arrangements for it to be brought back to England – this time overland.

The chap I hired said he would do the job for £500. He got the boat out of the water at Menton and on to the back of a low loader. Then on the outskirts of Menton, he hit a low bridge. Somehow or other he managed to get the boat under the bridge, but then had an engine failure in his towing unit. He had to limp back to England to get that repaired, leaving the boat on its low loader in a French layby for about three weeks. That did it no good at all. He eventually got it into Cherbourg, but there was a strike on, so he could not take it across the Channel.

By the time he got it back to Robin Knox-Johnston's yard in Poole, it was nearly a wreck. I was furious since he was supposed to be an expert haulier and I could see no reason why I should pay him £500 for wrecking my boat. Even with the £500, he said he would still be out of pocket on the job. Serve him right.

Anyway, Robin said to me (I think they all say the same, these yards): 'You can sell it for scrap for about £500 right now. On the other hand, I could give you two new engines, paintwork and some other work that wants doing. It'll cost you about £8,000 but, when it's finished, I reckon we can get £15,000 for the boat.'

I gave him the go ahead and, after about nine months, it was relaunched. It was no longer the same boat, so I told Robin to sell it. By this time I owed him £15,000 and he got £8,000 for the boat – completely reversing the figures he had quoted to me at the beginning! We wrote letters to each other for a long time about that.

Strangely enough, a very similar thing happened recently with our Stella sailing boat. Paul had sailed it to Greece – it took him three months – and he left it there for a while before sailing it back. Unfortunately, he got caught in a storm off Malta, the Stella was badly damaged and he left it on the island for the winter. I had to have it shipped back to the yard in Burnham-on-Crouch where it had been built, and the chap there told me exactly the same story. 'In its present state,' he said, 'I could get perhaps £3,000 for it, but by spending a couple of thousand more on it, I could probably get £5,500.' I told him to go ahead and so far the best offer he has had is £2,500. If I get anything back I will be lucky. That's the way boats are . . .

It is strange that, without any apparent effort, I am now talking about yachts and trips to the south of France, which must all sound very much like the good life. But it did not happen just like that. It was not a case of one day cycling around youth hostels in Germany and the next sailing my yacht in the Mediterranean. I cannot put my finger on any single moment in my life and say that this was the watershed as far as material possessions are concerned. The way I live now came about very gradually, and Rene and I have both had to work very hard for it all. There is no need to tell me that there is more to life than material possessions, either. I know that. I know it very well indeed.

CHAPTER ELEVEN

Rene Discovers the Algarve – and Reflections

DURING my story so far I have mentioned there were half a dozen times when I was fortunate enough to make the right decision regarding my own future, and the future of my business. Deciding to become a 'holiday tour organiser' in the first place was such a decision, of course, for I was under a great deal of pressure from my father to forget such nonsense and get a job as a tram driver. He had a friend on the trams and said he could fix it for me. It was a very good job, with prospects and a pension at sixty-five. But it is no good telling a youngster about prospects and pensions when he wants to find adventure, so I ignored his advice and took the plunge. As a matter of fact, he did not like me going to Germany on my cycle trips either, because he hated the Germans, as so many men did who had bitter memories of the First World War.

Anyway, that decision was a watershed in my life, as was the decision after the war to take up the travel business again instead of the tempting offer from the Foreign Office. There had been other decisions, too, but I have to put on record here and now that the best decision and the most inspired move was Rene's and not mine. It was she who 'discovered' the Algarve – that southern region of Portugal which I used to describe in my brochure as 'Europe's best kept secret' and whose popularity in the 1960s and 1970s boosted our fortunes tremendously. So if you have ever enjoyed a holiday down there do not thank me. Thank Rene.

I can tell you precisely when the Algarve adventure began. It was Christmas Eve, 1960, and we had a small party in our house in Upminster. Among the guests was a friend of ours called Vic Cowing. His father had had a little ironmonger's shop which Vic had built up into a fairly big business throughout Essex. He had just sold out and had ended up with something like £350,000, a colossal sum in those days. He had sent the bulk of it out of the country, and spent his evening telling all and sundry that he was going to emigrate. When I heard this, I assumed he meant Australia or Canada, which was where most people made for, but he told me he was aiming for a place called the Algarve. I had never heard of it.

'It's a fantastic place, Harry,' he told me. 'I've just been on a motoring holiday down through Portugal. I took the car all the way down there through France and Spain, and I've been away for a couple of months. The place I'm talking about is right down in the bottom left hand corner of Europe.'

Well, I thought about this for a moment, recalling my school geography, and worked out that he was talking about the south of Portugal. He went on to tell me about this fabulous area he had found and how he had made inquiries and finally bought a piece of land down there. He was going to emigrate, he said, and build villas on the land. And that was more or less that. I congratulated him and wished him luck, and the party went on its merry way.

The next day – Christmas Day – at 10 o'clock in the morning, there was Cowing ringing our doorbell, having brought over the plans for his 'development' down in the Algarve. Something that either I or Rene had said to him had led him to think that we were more than politely interested, so he had come over to show us what it was all about. For my part, I still could not work out exactly where he was talking about, and kept calling it 'the bottom left hand corner'. Being hospitable, we opened a couple of bottles of wine and looked at his plans. They were nothing more than a sketch of a lump of countryside five miles from the coast and some drawings of the kind of villas he wanted to build. It was as vague as that but, by the time he left us, Rene had bought the top of his hill! Like me, she had never heard of the place, but she liked the sound of it and paid Vic about £5,000 for the plot including a villa which he would build there.

I had absolutely no interest in the Algarve at all. Rene had been going on for some time about buying some land in the south of France, and that had not interested me either. After a couple of months, however, Vic came to see us and to tell us that the development was coming along well. He wanted to know if we would like to go down and look the place over.

'Not likely,' I told him. 'How would we get there?' He explained that it would mean flying to Lisbon and then taking a train down to the south. As a matter of principle I did not like going anywhere without an airport, so I said to count me out. But Rene was taken with the idea and went down there with Vic and his wife – just for the weekend. In fact, they drove down from Lisbon because Vic had a car there.

She came back bubbling with enthusiasm for the place. 'It's just like Ireland, but with sunshine, Harry,' she told me. 'It is really wonderful and we ought to think about selling holidays there.'

I remained unimpressed, mainly because there was no convenient airport, but Rene went back there several times over the next two years. After that, we began to send one or two customers there, mainly people who had property interests, and we also made travel arrangements for Vic Cowing and his friends and potential customers. But it was a very expensive operation taking people by plane to Lisbon and on by taxi to the south, and there was absolutely no question of mounting anything like a proper holiday operation.

All this time villas were being built at this place called Caravela, (which means a small boat in Portuguese, and I suggested it because of its similarity to Caravelle, the first jet aircraft we had chartered) and Rene's house was slowly taking shape. One day she came to me waving a letter she had received and informed me that her roof was about to be put on and we must both go there for the topping out ceremony. 'It's very important,' she explained. 'They do it in style and have a party, and you really ought to come.'

By now my curiosity was aroused, so even though I pretended not to be terribly keen, I was quite glad of the opportunity of looking over this part of the world about which Rene and Vic and several other people were raving.

I thought it was pretty good, too, although from the practical point of view, as a tour operator, I knew it would be of no interest to anyone because it did not have its own airport. I certainly did not want to offer holidays with a 200 mile transfer by car or coach or rail. We had had enough of that in Austria for so many years in the old days.

'But Harry, there is going to be an airport,' explained Vic. 'The authorities reckon they'll have it built at Faro in 1965.' (This, by the way, was 1963.)

'No, Vic,' I replied, with all the benefit of my tour operating experience. 'You can tell that to the marines. Airports are never built on time. If the authorities say 1965, you can bet your boots it'll be 1970, or even later.'

But, to my surprise, it was completed right on time and, in 1965 we were able to start flying holidaymakers to the Algarve to 'Europe's best kept secret'.

We shared an aircraft with the Lord Brothers – Stephen and Christopher – who ran a tour operating company at that time. It was a BAC 1-11 with 114 seats and we took 40 or 50 of those seats each week. At that time Lord Brothers were going great guns and would have no difficulty filling up the aircraft, or so they thought. In fact, it went rather slowly because there were hardly any hotels and the region had simply no experience of dealing with holidaymakers. I was interested only in the stretch of coastline which ran west from Faro towards Sagres, and, in that stretch, the only hotel that had recently been built was the Hotel do Garbe. Another had been there for many years in Praia da Rocha – a very old-fashioned house that belonged to one of the noble families of Portugal many years ago. The Hotel Eva in Faro itself was no more than a blueprint, so there was not much to choose from.

The do Garbe was owned by Dr Oliviera do Santos, who had come back from Angola with some money and invested it in this venture. He was an artistic sort of chap, but difficult to deal with because he wanted nothing at all to do with travel agents. He only had a few rooms and they were very easily sold, as he explained to Rene when she called on him.

The answer seemed to be to use some of the villas that had been built but whose owners were not in residence, and this is what brought me to a place called the Aldeia Turistica near Albufeira. It was a purpose built holiday village with apartments and villas and a small bar, as well as a local shop where visitors could buy provisions. It had been built by Sidney de Haan, the chap who had founded Saga Holidays, so I negotiated with him and obtained some villas there. They did quite well that summer, and the next, so I turned my thoughts to running the tour operation right through the winter as well.

In October of 1966 I went down to the Algarve to negotiate for some rooms at the new Hotel Eva, and also to the Aldeia Turistica to meet de Haan and talk over his plans for building an hotel. As we strolled among the villas in the warm autumn sunshine I asked de Haan where his clients were. He looked somewhat surprised and explained that the place had no clients outside the summer season. 'But Sidney, this is ridiculous,' I said. 'The weather is beautiful and the place is wonderful at this time of the year. Do you mean to tell me that there's nobody around except maids and gardeners and dogs?'

'Don't go on at me,' he replied. 'People just won't come here in the autumn and winter. They regard this as a summer destination and that's the end of it.'

To cut a long story short, I told Sidney de Haan that, if he gave me the villas at a cheap rate during the winter, I would fill them up for him, providing income and employment for the staff during that time.

'What would you call cheap?' he said.

'If you include maid service, I'd say £5 per person per week,' I told him.

He agreed on the spot and we shook hands on the deal. And that is how winter tourism in the Algarve began. As well as the Aldeia Turistica, we had beds in the Eva and in some villas at Montechoro to keep that BAC 1-11 busy. All we had to do was sell enough holidays to fill those aircraft seats and those beds. I talked it over with the Lord Brothers who agreed to join me in promoting autumn and winter holidays. On the strength of this, I chartered the BAC 1-11 for the winter of 1966/67, but the Lord Brothers then had to pull out of the deal, so Rene and I were faced with another of those 'shall we, shan't we?' decisions. Her enthusiasm for the Algarve prompted us to go it alone, and that turned out to be a great success.

Soon after this came another boosting factor for our winter business: the lifting of 'Provision One'. This had been a regulation of the Civil Aviation Authority that had prevented a tour company selling a package holiday abroad for less than the price of the normal return fare. The idea, I suppose, had been to stop business travellers buying holidays on charter flights in order to save money when they ought to have been buying ordinary air tickets on scheduled services. The travel trade had not liked the rule, because tour companies could easily have sold their holidays cheaper especially in winter, by virtue of their bulk-buying of aircraft seats and hotel beds.

By this time I was chairman of the Tour Operators' Study Group (TOSG) which consisted of the twenty leading holiday companies in the UK which carry about 5 million holiday-makers on package tours abroad every year. This group has exercised a considerable influence on the development of the package holiday to its present massive scale and it compaigned for two years to get rid of this minimum price control.

At last, in 1971 the CAA decided to relax the rule – in respect of winter holidays – and said the minimum price should not be below the *single* air fare. At that time the single fare to Faro was just £37 and we were able to offer a fortnight's holiday, including flights out and back for that sum. It was an incredible bargain and business boomed.

As year followed year, the story was the same: one of the steady growth in business to the Algarve. We got it up to three or four aircraft a week and, although other tour operators followed in our wake, I do not think anybody matched us. It all seemed set to go on without any hindrance, but then came one of those situations ever tour operator dreads – the outside force of politics disrupting the world of tourism. It had happened to me before, back in 1939 you will remember, and I had really hoped that it would never happen again. But we have no control over some aspects of our fate, and this was one of those uncontrollable, unforeseeable situations. Portugal had a revolution.

It happened in the April of 1974. It lasted from Wednesday 24th April to Saturday, 27th April, the shortest and most peaceful revolution on record. But what a birthday present! Others, far cleverer than I, have written about the Portuguese revolution, delved into the political implications and generally chewed over its bones. As a simple businessman, my concern was for my clients.

We had several hundred people down in the Algarve that week when the news broke. What primarily worried me was that the airports were closed and I had no way of knowing how I could get my people home. I thought at the beginning of it all that there would be no possibility of sending any more customers down, but as events worked out, that assumption was quite wrong. On the Saturday evening of the first week, 27th April, I heard from my contact in Lisbon – a friend who was constantly on the telephone to Upminster – that the airports might be opened again on the Sunday morning. We spoke half a dozen times during the Saturday, and very late that night he confirmed that Faro airport would, indeed, be opened at 5 am. I had my planes all standing by, ready to go, so alerted the airline's duty officer that it would be business as usual. He had heard nothing through the airlines' grapevine, so he bravely took my word for it and began assembling the crews.

1979: *An award from the Austrian Government, from their Ambassador in London. Left to right: Sidney Silver, Cosmos; H.E. the Ambassador; Roger Davis, Thomsons; Norbert Burda, Austrian Tourist Office; John Holding, Sovereign Holidays; Jorge Felner da Costa, Portuguese Tourist Office.*

1934–1984: *Back at Tower Bridge, not the same boat.* Co-operatzia *exchanged for* Iraine II.

1984: *Return to Cairo as courier.*

Meanwhile, Rene and I spent a long time telephoning our representatives down in the Algarve, telling them to get out and tell the customers that their homeward flights would be going as planned. The strange thing was that most of these customers had no idea at all what was happening. When the reps came to them with the news that all was well, they simply asked 'Why shouldn't it be'. They had had no newspapers and did not listen to the radio, so they had had no means of knowing what the situation was. The hotel staff, shop assistants and restaurant waiters – the only Portuguese they made contact with – were not inclined to discuss politics with foreign tourists, there had been no disturbances on the streets, no marches or demonstrations or anything like that. It was, as far as the Algarve was concerned, a very quiet revolution.

My other surprise was that clients who had booked to travel down to Portugal that day also turned up for their flights – well, most of them. Having paid for their holidays, they were unwilling to forgo them. We were also lucky in that many of the customers were frequent travellers to Portugal, and had faith in the people they knew. Of course, the news affected some people who were frightened off more by the stories in the British newspapers than by the facts of the situation (but that is nothing new), and those of our clients who did cancel, received a complete refund. However, most travelled as usual, especially those who had bought villas and apartments down there. Most tour companies maintained their flights through the summer because they had got the bookings before April, but the following season, the autumn/winter of 1974/75, was a disaster. All the tour companies cancelled their charter flights – not just the British companies, but the Germans and Scandinavians, too – and we had the strange experience of being the only company to run charter flights down there for something like six months. If you wanted a holiday in the Algarve, you went with the Travel Club of Upminster, and although the total number of people fell away by more than 50 per cent, we looked after those that remained. It was a remarkable season.

The hotels were affected, of course, because although they were virtually empty, they could not sack any of their staff. A communist regime had taken over in the initial stages (I suppose I ought really to say 'an extreme left wing' regime, because I do not think labels like 'communist' or 'conservative' are sufficient to describe political attitudes these days). One of the extreme measures the regime introduced in the first few weeks – before being slung out and replaced by one that was not so far to the left – was to bring in a minimum wage. It was about three times what the wage had been previously and, quite frankly, it needed to be so because wage levels down there were very low. They also introduced a system whereby the worker received a month's holiday with pay, and double pay in August and December – in effect receiving 14 months' salary for 11 months' work. The hotels were therefore saddled with huge wage bills, under-employed staff, and no guests. It was actually embarrassing to go into some of the hotels at that time. You would find you were the only couple in the bar, with three or four staff eager to serve you, or you would discover a dozen waiters hovering in the dining room with only a couple of tables occupied.

The hotel staff spent all their time talking politics – and my goodness how they made up for the years of suppression!

They talked and talked about the nuances of this policy or that, the effects of this course of action versus that, and where the country was heading. After fifty years of dictatorship, they went overboard on politics and, in my view, went too far the other way, spending too much time talking about the rights of free speech and the freedom to vote and form trades unions and that sort of thing. It was all heady stuff, but it was essentially irrelevant to the day-to-day problems of doing business and earning a living. What most annoyed me was the rash of graffiti on all the walls in the Algarve. All those lovely whitewashed walls were daubed and sprayed with symbols and slogans until the eye and the mind reeled. Politics are bad for the environment.

We had no problems, because I refused to get involved with political or union matters. I left all that to the good citizens of Portugal and the managers and owners of the hotels and apartment blocks. The only time it brushed against us was when the maids in the villas wanted to join unions and somebody telephoned me at the Caravela house to discuss the matter. This was, I think, an Englishwoman married to a Portuguese who had appointed herself a kind of semi-official spokeswoman for many of the tour company reps in the area (I think she worked for OSL). Anyway, she asked me if I would attend a meeting of all the maids and gardeners who wanted to adopt a policy in respect of their new union. I thanked her politely, told her I did not wish to attend the meeting and that, as a foreigner living in Portugal, I would not abuse the country's hospitality by getting involved in such matters. And that was that.

Other resident English people did get involved. As a result of the new conditions, we all had to meet higher wage bills, and as far as I was concerned it was no bad thing that these people were now earning decent money. However, very many of the old-style residents ('The Old Colonials' we used to call them) grumbled furiously. Their maid service had been costing them something like five pence an hour and now they were having to pay ten times that sum. They thought it scandalous. In my view it was nothing of the kind. They had been taking advantage of virtual slave labour conditions.

One chap who did get involved – I suspect against his will and his better judgement – was Henry Cotton, the legendary golfer and splendid character who has designed some superb golf courses around the world, and particularly down along the Algarve. He lives in a most beautiful house on the first tee of the Penina golf course (one of his designs, of course) and was highly revered, not just by golfers but by just about everybody along the Algarve. One of his business interests was the golf shop in the Penina club house, and he used local labour to help in one particular way. The caddies would collect lost balls for him, and he would pay them a few pence for every one they turned in. Then he employed other people – I think maybe it was a couple of old ladies – to scrub up the balls and make them look respectable. He would box them up in half dozens and sell them in the shop as 'seconds' for quite a good price. It was an arrangement that seemed to suit everybody involved, but when the revolution came, the hotel staff, the caddies and the old ladies all joined the union and got a little difficult. Now Henry Cotton is not the sort of man to stand for bolshie people, and he was a bit short tempered with their demands. The secretary of the union went to see him, arguing that Mr Cotton was earning a lot of money from the sale of second-hand golf balls, so the caddies and others deserved more than the few pence he was paying. What happened at this point is a matter of debate. The union chap claimed that Henry Cotton struck him, but Henry argues that he merely pushed him and told him to get out of the office.

You can probably guess the rest. All the staff went on strike and there was practically a second revolution in the Penina. Henry Cotton decided that he wanted none of this and so cleared off to Marbella and lived there for a couple of years. But time is a great healer and now he is back in the same house in Penina and all is now sweetness and light again.

Both Rene and I have a soft spot for the Algarve. We did well there from a business point of view, having things more or less our own way for a few years before other tour companies went there. But we also made a lot of friends in Portugal, and it is for that reason I was glad we were able to continue flying in and sending holidaymakers there during a time when the Portuguese were going through a traumatic experience.

I have now seen how the Algarve has developed over the years. I remember how it used to be, and compare that with the way it is today. Naturally I regret many of the changes, because I am as nostalgic as the next man. There are places that have become a sorry mess – the Alvor area, for instance, where eight or nine tower blocks, quite out of character, have been built near the beach. There are a few places like that, but on the whole I think the planners and the builders have not done to badly by the Algarve. They still have 200 miles of sandy beaches with nothing built on them, and a lot of regulations to protect beaches and other areas. Most of it is still untouched by the 20th century and I would echo Rene's description of it as 'Ireland with the sunshine' – but Ireland as it had been in the late 1800s.

It happens everywhere, and not just in Portugal, that argument about change and development and the growth of tourism affecting traditional lifestyles. People are always contending that places have been spoiled, and blaming the tour companies and the travel writers who encourage people to visit certain resorts and bring about the pressure for change. But for every person who objects to development and change, there is one who will welcome it – usually because he or she is on the receiving end of its benefits.

What the travel writer calls 'picturesque' can just as easily be called 'underdeveloped', what the newspaper or magazine article evokes as 'a lifestyle unchanged for centuries' or 'quaint local customs' is really another way of describing people who are living in poverty and lacking the amenities that we take for granted. The village well may look quaint and pretty in your holiday snaps, but you prefer to get your water from the tap in the kitchen, don't you?

As for the Algarve, the change wrought by tourism has overwhelmingly been for the better. The local people's standard of living has increased by leaps and bounds. More than 50 per cent of the population was illiterate twenty-five years ago. Now they have the schools they need and the children are benefitting as they should. Twenty-five years ago you saw young women and girls wearing the dark dresses and skirts that their grandparents wore, not for the sake of tradition, but because they had no alternative. Now they have the economic freedom of choice and dress in a way that would not be out of place in Oxford Street. Oh, they keep the old costumes for those special occasions, for the weddings and the festivals and the folkdancing, but the financial benefits of tourism have provided them with choice.

They have running water now, better sewerage and inside lavatories. Nobody had any running water or mains drainage at Caravela, where our friend Vic built his villas. The roads are better now, and it is a condition of future development that a builder will have to supply the whole place with mains drainage before a single brick is laid. Permission for building those first 20 villas all those years ago was only give when Vic agreed to provide mains water for the village, and that is the way it has been all along the Algarve. The provision of electricity often followed the same pattern. That is an aspect of 'tourist development' that the critics overlook.

Tourism has brought employment, too, and not just directly in the form of work in hotels, shops, restaurants, and so on. Some people argue that the traditional pursuits of fishing and farming have been neglected, but the tourists have provided a whole new market for the produce of the sea and the land. On balance, the Algarve has benefitted tremendously from the relatively new industry of tourism.

However, if the next question is: 'But are the local people happier as a result?' then I would have to bow out of the discussion, because metaphysical problems are not my cup of tea. Maybe they were happier when they led a simple life, because they knew of no other. But then you have to define what you mean by 'happy'. No, I shall simply say that their standards have improved, and there rest my case.

What more is there to tell you about Rene and me and the Travel Club of Upminster? Since the mid-1960s the expansion of our business into the

Algarve region of Portugal has occupied most of our time, although we did not neglect those other destinations in our brochure. We kept what we had on a fairly minor scale, however, sending more or less the same numbers each year to our favourite places in Switzerland and Austria, the Italian Lakes, Madeira, Tenerife, Crete and Majorca. We let the popularity of the Algarve carry our numbers up – but we made sure they did not get out of our control. As far as size is concerned, we are ticking over as usual with between 30,000 and 35,000 clients per year. Much depends on the size of the aircraft we have to use because, at the end of the day, it is a matter of putting backsides on aircraft seats and heads on hotel pillows. No matter how much they wrap it up with fancy jargon and no matter how big they get and how many grand experts they employ, all tour operators have to acknowledge that simple fact of life. It is hopeless to produce thick brochures and offer hundreds of thousands of holidays if you cannot get your load factor right – empty seats mean losses.

Rene and I have often talked this over and know that, with very little effort, we could quite easily double or treble the size of our business, but that would mean getting out of touch with it. We like to think we can control it all, with the help of a small staff on whom we can rely. We still see all the letters coming in and going out, just as we did in those far off days in Springfield Court. In fact, Rene opens the post in bed every day at 7 am sharp – and it comes by the sackful! Incidentally, one of the travel trade newspapers once asked if a photographer could come to Upminster and take a picture of Rene and me in our boardroom. 'You mean talking over the business?' I asked. 'A directors' meeting, as it were?' 'That is what they wanted, but the were quite put off when I said that we hold our conferences and our directors' meetings in bed (which is very convenient so long as you have only two directors)!

No, we think we are quite large enough at our present size and doubling the numbers does not mean doubling the profits. Quite the reverse. At present we can carry 35,000 passengers at 90% load factor on our capacity and show a handsome profit, but with 80,000 passengers representing 80% load on capacity, it would involve a massive loss. No thank you, we believe 'Turnover is vanity'; 'Profit is sanity'. Besides, we can treat our clients like human beings, instead of cyphers on a computer print-out.

It is not as if we are struggling to survive. Back in 1970, with our son Paul grown up and at university, and with the Algarve building up steadily, we had another little burst of spending. After all, the years had gone by with tremendous speed and we were living in fairly modest fashion despite Rene's investment in her Algarve villa.

We bought a new boat and a new car – a Jensen – and, by a great stroke of good fortune, we bought a penthouse in Park Lane. We had been renting a little one-room place in St. James's, but the lease ran out and there was no way we could renew it. This was a disappointment to me because it was in a first class situation. Now, many many years previously, when I was a £1-a-week office boy, I remember cycling along to the Marble Arch end of Oxford Street and looking at the smart penthouse apartments that had been built over the top floor of the Cumberland Hotel. It was my ambition to have one of those and I have to admit that this ambition remains unfulfilled. I had to settle for a place at the other end of Park Lane, down by Buckingham Palace!

When the St James's flat could no longer be kept, we searched around for something else and happened to see a flat for sale off Park Lane. We did not think we could afford it, but went along all the same. It was all right, but its enormous disadvantage was that it was on the tenth floor of a high block and was surrounded on all sides. In the front was the Inn on the Park, and you looked right into one of the bedrooms there. On the side was the Hilton – again with a view into somebody's bedroom. We asked the agent if there was something higher up, with a view, but he said all the higher flats had been sold.

Then, as we were leaving, he remembered that there was an uncompleted flat right at the very top. It had been reserved for the owner of the land as part of the price to be paid by the developer – so much in cash, plus a free flat – but the landowner had died, so the place was never finished. Up we went and clambered around this bare concrete shell. Rene looked at me, and I looked at Rene and we both decided there was something here worth pursuing. I telephoned the owners of the block who were eager to sell and immediately offered to knock £5,000 off the price. They assumed I knew the price, but I did not. All I did know was that £5,000 off anything was a bargain not to be missed. So I bought it without knowing what the price was. Yes, I know that is a stupid thing to do and I would never do such a thing in my normal business dealings. But, as I have said so often in my tale, there are times when you just have to take a deep breath and plunge in.

It turned out to be an enormous bargain. Believe it or not, we have since been offered ten times what we paid for it! The offer came from the agent of a Lebanese businessman who simply increased the price each time I said I was not interested in selling. He could not believe that I meant what I said, although I treated the whole thing as a joke until he made that offer. In the end I had to talk it over properly with him, because I knew there was an identical flat for sale in the block and could not understand why it had to be mine. It transpired that the businessman feared for his life and wanted my flat because it is not, and cannot be, overlooked because of the building regulations. All the other flats in the block and, indeed, in the area, are looked into from hotel bedrooms and the Lebanese chap feared that an assassin could get into one of them and take a pot shot at him. In my top floor eyrie he would be perfectly safe, with a couple of bodyguards at the top of the lift to vet all callers.

At that time all the Lebanese and other Arabs were flocking to that end of Park Lane because of the casinos and night clubs. They were walking around with thousands of pounds in their pockets, with their bodyguards and gambling like mad in the clubs and casinos. But that is something that has never interested me. I have never gambled because I reckon I do all the gambling I want with my business, juggling my aircraft seats and working out my charter needs and hotel requirements. That is enough gambling for me.

Talking about material possessions, let me tell you a story about the Jensen. We bought it, as I say, in 1970. A couple of years later we were invited to go down to the London docks for a party to be held on board a new Norwegian ship which was paying her first visit to Britain. We tend to get a lot of invitations to such functions and, as they are usually good parties, we accepted this one. Down we drove in the Jensen, right up to the dock and along the quayside. It was pouring with rain and, as we were dressed up to the nines, I was not looking forward to parking the car and legging it to the ship. Fortunately there was a young chap at the foot of the gangplank who smartly opened the door for Rene and told me to leave the keys in the ignition. 'I'll park it for you, sir,' he said.

Naturally I assumed he was a crew member detailed to do that duty, as there were lots of other cars parked neatly on the quay and several sailors running around. By now you have probably guessed that I was wrong.

The party broke up around three in the morning and I walked down the gangplank to see that every single car had gone. There was not a Jensen in sight. Back we went and found the purser to ask where his chap had parked my car. But he said he had not put any of the crew members on such a duty, and that was when the truth dawned on us.

We went to the police station where the sergeant gave us a cup of tea each, rang for a taxi, and took our address and phone number. 'It's quite commonplace, this sort of thing,' he said, in an attempt to be reassuring. 'The lads usually pinch a Rolls when they want a flash night out up West, especially if they're trying to impress a girl. Still, I suppose a Jensen's the next best thing.'

'You reckon some local lad took it, then?' I asked.

'No doubt about it, Mr Chandler,' he replied. 'But, then, you've got no idea what some of these East End villains are like.'

'I know all about East End villains, Sergeant,' I replied. 'I was a constable at Canning Town nick, long before your time.'

A couple of days later the police phoned to say the car had been found and was in the station yard just off Gray's Inn Road. It seemed to be no worse for wear but, as I was going to Switzerland a few days later, I took the opportunity of putting it into the garage to have some repairs done. One was to the radio which had developed a lot of crackling interference. Two or three days later I had a phone call in my Swiss hotel. It was the garage man who could hardly wait to tell me that I had provided him with a unique repair job, something he had never encountered with a Jensen before. The interference on the radio has been caused because a rat had built a nest in the boot and she and her two babies were happily munching through the electrical wires!

'Ah, they'll be London Dock rats,' I said. 'That'll teach me to park more carefully in future.'

Yes, 1970 was a year when we had something of a splurge, buying a boat and a car and that flat off Park Lane. The only other thing we have bought of note since then is another villa in the Algarve – a property in the Vale do Lobo development. Rene says that we are the only couple she knows who have 'his' and 'her' villas – one at each end of the Algarve! Rene is also the only person I know who has two swimming pools and cannot swim, and she says I am the only man with two boats who gets seasick.

I realise that I am not easily identifiable as a socialist – but that is what I am, or was until a few years ago. I know I have all the trappings of a bloated capitalist – the properties, the boat, the posh car – and Rene reckons I am the sort of chap who would have ground down the workers if I had been born a hundred years previously! But I am a socialist at heart, and always will be. As a youngster I was a communist. I had seen the hunger marchers coming down to London from Jarrow yet I was reading in the newspapers at the same time that in Brazil and other South American countries they had a glut of coffee and wheat and were burning it in order to maintain the prices. I could not square that, just as I cannot square the present situation, with millions starving in Third World countries and the Common Market bloated with its surplus food – its butter and meat mountains and its lakes of milk. For God's sake, why not use the surpluses to feed the hungry? The European economy would not suffer, for the farmers have been paid for the stuff.

Of course it was very fashionable to hold communist beliefs in the 1930s. I was not a university graduate, I was struggling to make my way out of the East End, but many of my contemporaries in the universities became communists. Some of them were the Philbys and the Burgesses who crossed the line from idealistic, honest communism to treachery. But many thousands did not, and despite the strength of the Peace Pledge movement and that Oxford Union debate about not fighting for King and Country, a lot of them did fight the great evil of National Socialism as preached and practised by Herr Hitler and his gang.

Ironically, it was in the wartime conditions a few years later that I saw the theory of communism working well – in the kibbutzim of Israel. But in the long run, and in normal peacetime conditions, it just does not work in practice. Human nature would have to be changed before people were ready for communism.

I became a socialist and have been ever since, although I have to set aside my political opinions when I am running my business. The trouble with many socialists is that they do not know how to run businesses!

I have to admit that during the past ten years, I have suffered if not a conversion, then a suspension of belief. I voted Conservative in the last two elections because, like Churchill in 1940, I felt that they had the right person in the right place at the right time.

I grew up listening – at street corner meetings and in the House of Commons – to people like Clement Attlee, Stafford Cripps, Herbert Morrison, Ernest Bevin, Aneurin Bevan, George Lansbury, Beveridge, Walter Citrine and Frank Cousins, and they made an enormous impression on me. What a contrast then to hear in recent years on the radio people like the ineffectual Kinnock or Hattersley or, worse, the odious Heffer, Scargill, Skinner and Kaufmann who rant and rave in a manner I have not heard since Hitler fifty years ago. Then there is the infantile behaviour in the House, the baying noises of their supporters when they stop for breath, drowning the Speaker's plaintive calls to Order. One can only hope that this spectacle is never brought to the television screen to further lower the respect in which Parliament has always been held.

All this over recent years has brought me to the conclusion that the current Socialist Party leaders are not of the calibre to offer a credible alternative government for many years to come. Maybe I shall have to think again at the next election.

A note from John Carter
Thus far, Harry Chandler has told his own story in his own words with, I trust, an acceptable amount of 'editorial re-structuring' by me!

Because I felt that the story was best told by him (after all, he is the one who has lived it), I regarded the setting down of it as my main task.

But not my only task. For we have now reached a point where Harry Chandler has to be properly set into the wider context of his time and his trade – in particular, we have to examine the influence he has had on the popular holiday business in Britain and abroad during the last twenty years.

This is a story he cannot tell himself and although he had provided me with a lot of the background material, he now leaves centre stage and, metaphorically, takes a seat in one of the boxes. I have no doubt he will contribute his comments from time to time – it would be unlike Harry to remain silent.

But, if you'll excuse me, Mr C., I'll take up the story from here . . .

Telephone: ALB 1554.

H. W. CHANDLER
TRAVEL AGENT
c.
ORGANISER AND HOST - BRITISH AND
CONTINENTAL HOLIDAY PARTIES.

25 HERMIT ROAD,
LONDON · E·16.

*Agent for Leading Tourist Agencies
and all British Holiday Camps.*

To all ex-students and friends of
THE GROVE SCHOOL

February, 1939.

SARNEN : BERNESE OBERLAND
15 DAYS Inclusive Holiday, 10 GUINEAS.

Departures :   June 3rd and 24th.   July 15th.
                     August 5th and 26th.   September 9th.

Sarnen is a small medieval town which still retains its rural Swiss character, and is situated on the northern end of a lake of the same name in the Bernese Oberland. Lake Sarnen is beautifully placed some twenty miles south of Lucerne, and between the Lake of Lucerne and Lake Thun, on which stands Interlaken.

We are staying at the Hotel Waldheim, about twenty minutes' walk along the lake side from Sarnen. Picture if you can a chalet, deep-set in trees, with smooth lawns and flower beds sloping gently down towards the crystal-clear waters of Lake Sarnen ; around for a thousand square miles stretches the mighty expanse of snow-covered peaks which form the Pennine Alps and the Bernese Oberland. This will give you some idea of the fine situation of the Hotel Waldheim on Lake Sarnen.

Here are facilities for every kind of enjoyment, active and otherwise. Boats and punts are available for excursions to other lake-side villages, whilst swimming and sun-bathing enthusiasts can go straight from their rooms to the Hotel beach in their bathing costumes. Fishing is also available. Excellent walking country commences on the very doorstep of the Hotel, on the slopes of the majestic Pilatus, and in early summer these slopes are literally carpeted with Alpine flowers and quaint primitive ferns. Within the limits of one-day excursions are Interlaken, with the mighty Jungfrau, the Reichenbach Falls, the finest in Switzerland, and the tour that is claimed as the most magnificent in Europe, that over the passes of the Central Swiss Plateau, the Furka, the Grimsel and the Axenstrasse to the world-famous Rhone Glacier. The mighty peaks of the Pilatus, the Rigi and the Stanserhorn ranging up to 12,000 feet are all within reach for those with a taste for mountaineering, the ubiquitous funicular railway offering transport to the " not so active " members of the party.

The price of 10 Guineas includes the following items :—

Return travel London, Dover, Ostend, Strasbourg Bale, Lucerne (III class)
Coach or rail to the Hotel.
Reserved seats throughout.
Breakfast in Bale and Lunch in Lucerne on the outward journey
Dinner in Lucerne on the return journey
Hotel accommodation and full board.
All tips to servants and Government taxes.

These parties will definitely be limited in number, and accompanied throughout by myself. I am convinced that at Sarnen we have the ideal centre for Switzerland, and I believe I shall convince you too.

One of our early brochures.

PART 2

CHAPTER TWELVE

Into Context

TO PUT Harry Chandler into 'the context of his time and his trade' I go back to the summer of 1964, which is more or less when I first met him and certainly the first time I became aware of his influence. A travel company called Fiesta Tours had gone spectacularly bust in the July of that year and a lot of people in the industry were running around like headless chickens, worrying about the damage it would do to their collective credibility. As Fiesta had not been a member of the Association of British Travel Agents (ABTA), it had had no legal responsibility to its customers. Nevertheless the newspapers were busy tarring everybody with the same brush – after all, it was summer and the collapse had come right in the middle of a slack period as far as news was concerned.

Like other journalists, I wrote about the plight of the stranded Britons abroad, and the chagrin of those who had paid Fiesta for holidays, but were now not going to get them. Asked privately by friends in the industry for my views on what ABTA should do, I said that, for the sake of future goodwill, the association should at least try to bring home the stranded holidaymakers and not shelter behind the letter of the law.

It was then that Harry Chandler came into the picture, taking action which was to focus attention dramatically on what needed to be done, and demonstrating that he, for one, was doing something. He flew to Perpignan in the company of Mr Godfrey Lagden, his local Member of Parliament. They found hundreds of British holidaymakers thronging the airport – 'just like a refugee camp,' Harry said. These people had no money to get home, but Harry had some empty seats on a returning charter flight, so put as many on board as he could. Touring other resorts, he showed Lagden, and press photographers and reporters just what kind of rescue operation was needed.

This brought swift results. Back in London, the ABTA president, Charles 'Tubby' Garner, demonstrated that under his ample and jovial exterior, there was a man of action and he mobilised members to provide similar help.

In time, Godfrey Lagden was able to tell colleagues in the House of Commons that not all tour companies were tarred with the same brush. His support for the trade was to prove useful in the aftermath.

There was an understandable call for holidaymakers to be given some sort of protection from the likes of Fiesta, for it had not been the only holiday company to fail in such fashion. The early 1960s produced a crop of them – some genuine firms who simply could not cope, but too many run by crooks who were out to fleece the public. It was clear that something would have to be done. Pressure for action became even stronger a few weeks later when a firm called Omar Khayyam failed, again leaving a legacy of dashed hopes and angry customers.

The government of the day began making noises about some sort of licensing scheme to control the travel trade and, at its annual conference in Brighton towards the end of the year, Trade Secretary Roy Mason gave ABTA an ultimatum. Shorn of the pleasantries – for Roy Mason is a pleasant sort of chap – it amounted to: 'If you don't sort yourselves out, the government will do it for you'.

The last thing the trade wanted was government controls, and once again it was Harry Chandler who came up with a solution. He had, in fact, submitted a plan for some sort of protection scheme back in the April of 1964, long before Fiesta and Omar Khayyam had hit the deck, but with the knowledge of other, smaller failures and of the need to protect both customers and trade. In a letter to Ray Barker, then chairman of the Association's tour operators' committee, Harry outlined a scheme which he called 'reciprocal booking'.

In sum, the plan was that members of the Association would agree to trade only among themselves. Travel agents would sell only those holidays produced by tour operators who were members and tour operators, for their part, would sell only through member agents.

The Association's secretary, Richard Colmer, had been considering a similar plan put to him by one of his colleagues on the secretariat, Edgar Sadgunn; as 1965 got into its stride, the idea of reciprocal booking was dissected and discussed. Desmond Hopkinson took over from Garner as ABTA president, but the two of them worked closely on selling the plan to the trade. Apart from being longtime friends, 'Tubby' and 'Hoppy' were well known and well liked figures, but it took all their skills of diplomacy to persuade members that the plan was in their best interests. Hopkinson, in several speeches to regional meetings, kept hammering home the point that it would bring stability to the trade. Because of this, the scheme was named 'Operation Stabiliser' and, under the name, was put forward for approval at the 1965 conference in Jersey.

Throughout the months that had gone before, Harry Chandler had been lobbying tirelessly for the scheme and, as a reporter at that Jersey conference, I watched him working for its acceptance. There was considerable opposition, particularly from the small travel agents, who saw it as some plot to take business away from them.

To avoid any accusations of creating a closed shop, ABTA had to lower its standards of entry and this, too, was a cause of bitter debate. As a member of the ABTA council, Harry spent hours talking to delegates in and out of the conference hall. Like his colleagues on the council he was committed to it, but nobody was more committed than Hopkinson. When the debate ended, a vote was taken in an atmosphere of great tension. No issue had divided the trade as this one had done and many harsh words had been hurled around in the heat of the debates.

The result was announced – the conference had approved the Stabiliser plan. Hopkinson strode from the stage and, once out of sight of the delegates, broke down, weeping with emotion.

Is it not strange how people get emotional about matters which, to an outsider, can seem mundane? Looking back the Association really had no alternative but to go with the Stabiliser plan, for if the Jersey conference had rejected it, the government would have imposed its own regulatory system on tour operators and high street travel agents. In time a licensing system was imposed on tour companies, but we shall get to that by and by. Stabiliser remains in force to this day, having survived an expensive legal action against it, brought by the Office of Fair Trading. The Restrictive Practices Court held that Stabiliser was not against the public interest.

This episode was very material to the Harry Chandler story. One of the bitterest exchanges of the Stabiliser debate concerned the position of people like him – not that there were many – who sold their holidays direct to the public. Travel agents, knowing that Stabiliser would cut them off from several sources of commission, argued that tour operator members (eg Harry Chandler) should be required as a condition of membership to sell through agents and pay commission. If Chandler was not prepared to do this, he was told, he should resign. Some of that bitterness remains to this day.

For all his years as a member of ABTA, his work on its committees and councils and his work in the creation of the Tour Operators' Study Group (that is something else we shall come to later), Harry Chandler has never been honoured with the presidency of the Association. A demonstration, in my opinion, of the collective strength of small minded small men.

But let us move on a couple of years. To the annual conference of 1967 which was held in Bournemouth. In the weeks preceding it, some tour companies had been approached by a large travel agency chain seeking favourable trading terms – increased commission on sales. Each tour company had been told that, if it did not comply, its sales would suffer, and broad hints were dropped that some companies had already agreed to pay the higher rates. As competition between the companies was so tough, there was no easy way for any one of them to check on the true situation. Harry Chandler got to hear of this and, being the chairman of the Tour Operators Council and somebody who did not pay commission anyway, was in a position to bring the tour companies together to talk over that specific issue.

At a business breakfast in a Bournemouth hotel he did just that, persuading his fellow tour operators to lay their cards on the table. As a result, they called the bluff of the agency chain.

The same group later made what Harry was to call a 'foolish and quixotic decision' just after the conference when the pound was devalued. At a second meeting they decided not to impose currency surcharges, but to keep prices at the levels printed in their brochures and suffer heavy losses as a result.

The idea of regular meetings took hold and a handful of tour companies formed what was to become the Tour Operators' Study Group (TOSG), whose present membership of 20 or thereabouts encompasses all the biggest companies. As its founder, Harry Chandler was its longtime chairman and is now its president. He has had constantly to deal with critics inside and outside the business who look upon TOSG as some sort of travel trade Mafia, meeting secretly to carve up the cake for themselves. Travel agents are particularly suspicious of the group's activities.

In fact, the companies who form the group remain business rivals and refuse to discuss their own commercial affairs at the group meetings. As far as they are concerned, TOSG exists to lobby governments at home and abroad, to settle matters of mutual concern and act on a level that is, for want of a better phrase, above the plane of business. Thus, it is a TOSG delegation that will fly off to Madrid or Lisbon or Athens to lobby a Ministry of Tourism about the imposition of some tax or about a change in the law that affects their activities. It is, for example, TOSG which fixes the date on which brochure exchange rates are based, so bringing a measure of unity to price calculations.

And it was TOSG – with Harry Chandler at the helm – which produced another line of defence for the holidaymaker: a scheme which safeguarded the customers and once more protected the trade from the eager interference of government.

Following Fiesta's collapse, the idea was mooted that a fund should be created from which the victims of future failures could be compensated. The establishment of such a common fund was part of the 'Operation Stabiliser' plan, but its total never amounted to much. The main drawback was that tour companies were reluctant to contribute to any fund that would underwrite their competitors. Harry Chandler spent a lot of time seeking an alternative method of providing protection. As well as flatly refusing the common fund solution, tour companies argued that it was impossible to get guarantees against insolvency from the 'Big Five' banks. This was true as an agreement had been enforced for many years between the Central Clearing Banks that they would in no circumstances give any kind of bond or guarantee against commercial debts, although that guarantee is no longer in force. But Chandler refused to believe there was no solution and, in the end, his quest took him to the London offices of the Swiss Bank Corporation.

From them he learned that he could deposit any sum of money with them and receive in exchange an 'irrevocable letter of credit' for the same amount. In the event of his business failing, that deposited sum would be paid by the bank to some designated third party. Without properly realising it, he had stumbled upon a bonding system that would enable each tour operator individually to provide a financial safeguard for his own customers – if he was financially sound – without supporting his competitors. Furthermore, it was economic for the tour operator as he collected the interest on his cash deposit.

Although he has often described TOSG as a more efficient body than ABTA – 'ABTA must be democratic, but that slows everything up' – and although the members of TOSG are usually able to make decisions without having to refer back to their respective companies, it nonetheless took two dozen meetings and two years before the group was able to thrash out an agreement on a bonding system that satisfied each of its members and their lawyers.

So, on August 6th, 1970, at a press conference held in the Waldorf Hotel, Harry Chandler was able to announce a scheme to protect the holidaymaking public. The 22 members of TOSG had each obtained a bond, or guarantee, which was the equivalent of five per cent of annual turnover. The total amount of bond monies came to well over £5 millions.

'We don't think any member of TOSG needs such a guarantee,' declared Chandler. 'This is why we think we're the best people to start such a scheme, and we very much hope that others in the industry will follow.'

A journalist stood up to ask why ABTA had not come up with this scheme. Why had it been left to the 'Mafia' of TOSG to produce it? Harry Chandler explained that he had, in fact, proposed the bonding scheme to the ABTA council in 1967, but it had been rejected because it proved impossible to gain the agreement of the hundreds of members of ABTA to any scheme.

The press welcomed the idea and wrote about the travel trade 'coming of age' in respect of consumer protection. Others claimed it was the 'biggest advance in consumer protection in any service industry'. Talking years later with Harry Chandler about this period, I got something of an insight into the man's simple and straightforward approach to this and other problems – an approach which tends to produce results.

Having told me about his arrangement with the Swiss Bank Corporation, he said that a little later on he had decided to work instead with a merchant bank – Kleinwort Benson. 'I'd never heard of them,' he confessed, 'but I arranged to go to their offices in Fenchurch Street and, when I was going up on the train, I began to worry about who these people were with the peculiar foreign name. I didn't know if I could trust them with my deposit of £100,000. As I as turning this over in my mind, I read in the *Financial Times* that they had just advanced £100 millions, or some such incredible sum, to the Shah of Iran. They were giving him money to buy fighters for his air force. So I decided that if they were that big, my £100,000 would be safe enough. They gave me a splendid lunch in their board room and I was so impressed that I happily handed over my cheque without a care in the world!'

The one imperfection with the original TOSG scheme was that tour companies used customers' deposit money to pay for their bonds, making themselves even more dependent on an early cash flow. When the scheme was widened to include all tour companies and formed part of the licensing system run by the Civil Aviation Authority from 1973, it was made a condition that the bond should be funded from capital. The CAA has the right to scrutinise company accounts to ensure that bonds are adequate.

In 1974, however, the bonding system faced its first major crisis with the collapse of Court Line and the failure of the tour operating giant Clarksons. It was a time when Harry Chandler found himself once again at the centre of events. And when he found himself mixed up with politicians, and he did not much care for the experience.

In the early part of 1974 there had been several rumours around the travel trade regarding the viability of Clarksons. As part of the Court Line empire, it was a giant among tour operating companies, aiming to be the biggest and taking on all comers, including the well-breeched Thomson Holidays. As the two giants slugged it out, profit margins were shaved to the minimum and observers of the scene, recalling the troubles of a decade previously, warned darkly that no good would come of it. But the price war continued and the Court Line/Clarksons bandwaggon rolled on. The airline part of the business (Court Line) bought the giant Tristars and boasted about filling them more or less round the clock, ferrying holidaymakers down to the Mediterranean at rock bottom prices. Clarksons had absorbed other travel companies, including Horizon, whose founder Vladimir Raitz enjoyed a high reputation in the business – so much so that travel agents voted his company their number one favourite a short while before Clarksons took it over. Court Line invested in Caribbean hotels. And all the while sages shook their heads and waited for the collapse that seemed inevitable.

All round the country, travel agents were discreetly persuading customers to book holidays with other companies. They also held back deposits and bookings for Clarksons and, as June came along, it seemed that it would only be a matter of time before Clarksons folded up – if for no other reason than that the Tristars were inflexible and too big for the package holiday market at that time.

All this, of course, was kept within the confines of the trade. Journalists who questioned the viability of Clarksons were assured that everything was just fine. As far as the general public was aware, all was well.

Then, on June 26th, 1974, the Secretary of State for Industry, Mr Antony Wedgwood Benn, rose to his feet in the House of Commons and made a statement about Court Line Limited.

'As the House will know, Court Line, which owns shipyards and Clarksons and Horizon Tours, has approached the government for assistance to deal with financial difficulties which might have threatened employment in the shipyards and the order book for ships and the many hundreds of thousands of people now booked to go on holiday tours this summer,' he began.

'The government are ready to acquire the entire shipbuilding and ship-repairing interests of Court Shipbuilders and consider that this should stabilise the situation in respect of Court Line's interests, including the holidays booked for this summer. Future details are being worked out, and I will make a fuller statement as soon as possible.'

There was a strong reaction to this from the Conservative opposition and, in reply to a question from Mr Heseltine, Mr Benn declared: 'It was thought right that holidaymakers who had holidays booked this summer should have some reasonable security, and the government was anxious to help them.'

The public and the travel trade interpreted the government's action and Mr Benn's words as a guarantee that Court Line's troubles were over and holidays were safe. The travel agents happily sent off the deposits they had been holding and just as happily recommended Clarkson and Horizon holidays to their customers.

During the first or second week in July, I remember telephoning one of my better informed contacts and asking for his assessment of the Clarksons/Horizon situation. 'Everything in the garden's lovely' he said, quoting Marie Lloyd's old music hall song.

But everything in the garden was far from lovely, as Harry Chandler was to discover on August 9th.

It was a Friday and he was about to set off from Upminster for a weekend on his boat – a weekend away from the pressures of high summer when tour companies are rushed off their feet. But the telephone rang. His caller was his old friend from army days and after, George Skelton, who had risen high in the ranks of Pickfords and was, moreover, the current president of ABTA.

'George was ringing from the Board of Trade and he wanted me to attend a meeting there. I assumed he meant on the following Monday morning, as it was getting late, but he said he meant straight away. He wouldn't tell me what it was about, only that it was a matter of grave urgency. As chairman of TOSG, he said, I had no alternative but to join him. I knew George well enough to realise that something big was afoot.'

At the Board of Trade, Skelton was able to reveal that the meeting concerned the financial weakness of Clarksons. 'They called me in as

ABTA president, Harry,' he said. 'But as soon as I discovered what it was about, I told them my experience was as a retail agent and that they should get you in straight away. Clarksons are going under. Nothing can stop it.'

In conditions of the strictest secrecy, the two men conferred with Board of Trade officials into the late evening. At last a plan was drawn up that would keep Clarksons going until the end of September, thus reducing the liability on its £3.3 millions bond held by TOSG. The plan needed the approval of the Secretary of State for Trade, Mr Peter Shore, but he was in Singapore. Nonetheless the Board's officials seemed to think he would accept the proposals, and both Skelton and Chandler left the building expecting that the secret could be kept for the next six or seven weeks.

On the morning of Thursday, August 15th, Harry Chandler took a telephone call from the Board of Trade. Shore had returned and had accepted the plan. At 5 pm he took another call summoning him once more to Government offices – this time the Civil Aviation Authority. Lawyers had looked at the plan and advised Peter Shore that it could not be permitted. By the end of September, the Clarksons/Horizon debt would have increased by a million pounds. Knowing the inherent financial weakness of the company, it would be unlawful to allow it to continue trading. Chandler and Skelton suggested that a guarantee of debt payment from the company's bond or from ABTA might overcome that situation. The suggestion was turned down. The Secretary of State insisted that Court Line companies must cease trading immediately and go into bankruptcy.

In law, Peter Shore had had no choice but to make the decision he did. The company was insolvent. But he could not have chosen a worse day to pull the rug out from under the holiday companies. It was the peak of summer, with several thousand holidaymakers already abroad and several thousands more about to fly off in the next two days.

Harry Chandler returned to his Park Lane penthouse and made a handful of telephone calls. By nine o'clock that evening the directors of the TOSG Trust Fund were assembled there, all of them managing directors of the largest tour operating members of TOSG, together with the essential lawyers. The Clarksons/Horizon bond had to be called in and their customers brought home. They worked through the night, making countless telephone calls, each man drawing on the goodwill of colleagues, submerging rivalries, asking favours and sometimes twisting arms. By 5 am on Friday, August 16th, they had arranged for eleven flights to bring home Clarkson and Horizon customers. The first flight, a DC10 set off at 6 am to collect passengers from the cruise ship *Delphi*, docked at Sicily at the end of a Clarkson cruise. By midday the bond of £3.3 millions had been called in from the four banks involved in the bond and placed into a special account, ready to pay for the rescue operation and the subsequent demands. During the next ten days, 35,000 holidaymakers were brought home at a cost of £1 million. The balance of the bond was intended to compensate those who had paid for holidays but had been unable to travel because of the collapse. But it was not enough.

'We worked from Park Tower all through the night and at two or three in the morning of Friday, August 16th we moved over to Sun Street in the City of London, where Clarksons had their headquarters,' recalls Harry. 'We got the keys and let ourselves into the building in order to go through the files. I remember I went into the lavatory and on the back of the door I spotted a notice signed by the managing director who had only recently been appointed with the brief of saving the company. In his own handwriting it said "In the interests of economy, will the last man out please switch off the lights". Well, the lights had been switched off in Sun Street, with a vengeance.'

Like many others, Harry is still bitter at the way the politicians handled the Court Line affair, the way they interfered with the rescue operation and what they did afterwards 'for political expediency' – to save political face.

At one point, the Foreign Office contacted ABTA concerning the thousands of Britons stranded in Spain. ABTA reassured worried Whitehall that those Britons would be brought home and all the hotel bills paid from the bond, forgetting to mention that it was TOSG members who were mounting the rescue operation. The Foreign Office told our Ambassador in Madrid and he, in turn, reassured worried holidaymakers and hoteliers. Money from the bond, he told them, would be used to rescue all holidaymakers and pay their bills.

Unfortunately, the Spanish hoteliers interpreted this as meaning that all Clarkson and Horizon debts would be paid – which ran into many millions – not simply those incurred from the date of bankruptcy, as was the case under the terms of the trust fund. For two or three days the confusion remained, with the Foreign Office and the Board of Trade batting the problem around and TOSG watching from the sidelines.

On August 22nd, Peter Shore summoned the directors of the TOSG trust fund to a meeting in the House of Commons. Harry recalls it as if it were yesterday:

'We were called up there at nine o'clock in the evening and there was Peter Shore with all his officials. He told us Spanish hotels had seized people's luggage and were claiming payment for debts incurred before the bankruptcy. He said it was very embarrassing and that we would have to pay off debts from an earlier date, from about August 1st, when these holidaymakers had arrived in Spain, so they would be able to leave – to come home with their baggage.

'We told him we could not do this as it was not within the terms of the trust fund, but he insisted it had to be done "for political reasons", and added "I am giving you instructions". He also said it was a political matter out of our control.

'So we then told him we would do as he instructed – if he gave us an indemnity to cover any future action brought against us. We did not intend to suffer in any way as a result of doing something we knew to be illegal. He said he would give us such an indemnity on behalf of the government and, the following day, I received a letter to that effect, brought by government messenger to my home in Upminster.'

The political reasons Peter Shore mentioned stemmed from the fact that a general election was due in two or three weeks, and the government wished to be seen as the protector of the British holidaymaker. As soon as they received their indemnity, the directors of the TOSG trust fund sent one of their members off to Spain with a suitcase full of pesetas. He toured the Costas and the Balearic islands, paying off hotel accounts left, right and centre, but only for clients still on holiday at that time.

This established the principle that remains in force to this day that the bond would pay the entire hotel account for all clients of the failed company, not only from the date of the failure which is strictly in accordance with the terms of the trust fund, but also for the week or two before the failure back to the beginning of each clients' holiday when the collapse happens in the middle of it.

What the bond does not pay are the old debts of the failed companies for holidays already completed before the collapse. These are of course simply commercial debts and not covered by the bond but this misunderstanding still causes ill-feeling amongst hoteliers involved in every failure to this day.

The Court Line crash had two major repercussions, both political. The government had made a pre-election pledge to compensate those who had paid for but not gone on holidays. They did this by creating the Air Travel Reserve Fund – a unique institution on the British commercial scene.

The concept that future customers of successful companies should pay a levy in order to compensate the past customers of companies which had failed is, indeed, an amazing one. But it stemmed from amazing political circumstances.

During the debate on the fund in February of 1975, the Conservative opposition had claimed that the fund was being created to get Mr Wedgwood Benn off the hook. His words of the previous June had been widely interpreted as a guarantee that holidays were safeguarded. Norman Tebbit was particularly cutting: 'The Bill need never have come to us, at least in this form, but for the fact that the Secretary of State for Industry recklessly induced people to part with their money to a company which, when he spoke as he did, he either knew, or ought to have known, was not financially sound.' And later: 'The Bill is concerned with saving ministers from the consequences of statements so reckless that if they had made them in the normal course of business they might have been open to prosecution.'

The ATRF was to be started with a loan of £15 million from the Treasury to be repaid by a levy on future holidaymakers, an idea which was quite abhorent to the tour operators. As chairman of TOSG Chandler had written to every Member of Parliament and lobbied vigorously throughout the passage of the Bill to persuade the Government to provide the £15 million as a grant rather than a loan on the grounds that the Government should accept their responsibility for the extent of the loss of public money.

But to no avail and the ATRF was created and still exists – a 'political levy provided by customers of the travel trade'.

The other political consequence of the crash was the report in July 1975 by the Parliamentary Commissioner for Administration – the Ombudsman. A number of MPs had passed to him complaints from constitutents that they had been misled by Mr Benn's June statement interpreting it as an assurance that they could safely book their holidays with the Court Line companies. The Ombudsman concluded that Mr Benn had given that impression and that 'the government cannot be absolved of all responsibility for holidaymakers' losses arising from the Court Line collapse . . .' But the government ignored the report.

But all that is water under the bridge and enough time has passed for Harry Chandler and his colleagues to look back philosophically on the antics of the politicians and what they had said in the House of Commons. In the ATRF debate, Eric Deakins, then under-Secretary of State for Trade, described TOSG as: '. . . a collection of complacent, smug, self-satisfied, holier-than-thou tradesmen putting on airs and graces above their station in life,' but then hastened to assure the House that they were nothing of the kind.

'We wondered at the time whether to protest at what he called us,' recalls Harry with a wry smile. 'But we decided that, coming from a politician, we'd regard it as a compliment. And at least it seemed to indicate that our lobbying had had some effect on the House of Commons.'

CHAPTER 13

Rags to Riches

W E TALKED in Upminster and in Park Lane, Harry Chandler and I. And, as his story unfolded, I recalled other conversations we had enjoyed during the past twenty years or so, at press briefings and luncheons, in the hurly-burly of ABTA conferences and in the comparative tranquility of the Algarve. And I reflected that the man has changed hardly at all since our first meeting – although a villainous looking eyepatch he sometimes sports is proof of one physical change and the aftermath of a series of operations in 1977 and 1983.

In May of 1977, a couple of weeks after his 64th birthday, Harry suffered a heart attack and the following month went into hospital for an operation to remove a cataract on his left eye. July saw him back in hospital as a result of a second heart attack, spending three weeks in an intensive care unit. That would have been enough for any man, but Harry jokes that he doesn't do things by halves and, in August, he had to be treated for a more serious condition in his left eye, a detached retina. Just to round off his summer, September brought his third heart attack.

Now in case you think I am dismissing casually what was a most serious phase in Harry Chandler's life – what, indeed, could have been the end of Harry Chandler's life – I am treating it in this way because that is the way he himself treats it. I have no doubt that at the time the state of his health completely dominated the lives of Harry and Rene Chandler and their son Paul, and even now Harry is aware of how serious it all was.

'Rene was given some very grave opinions from the doctors,' he told me. 'They wondered if I would even survive and said that, if I did, I would have to take it easy. They ruled out flying, for example. They said I'd never be able to go in a plane again.'

But Harry Chandler, who even now at 72 is spry and sprightly, had always kept himself fit. Until that summer he had skied regularly, and it was the basic strength of his constitution that pulled him through. He has proved the doctors wrong by continuing to fly to whichever part of the world his business interests take him. He continues to work long hours, often seven days a week, devoting an average of two to three days a week to work on behalf of ABTA and TOSG. When I have tackled him about taking it easy, as the doctors ordered, he just waves the idea aside and, like so many others of his temperament, explains that, if he did not have half a dozen things on the go at once, he would become bored and stagnate. 'If I have to go away for a couple of days, I usually come up here and work through the weekend,' he says, indicating the room in which we sat, on the top floor of his Upminster home. Under the eaves is Harry's den, with personal files stacked along the walls, a bright eyed word processor on a desk by the window and a clutter of papers and telephones on the desk. The middle of the room is taken up by a full size billiards table, covered with boards, on which more files and folders are strewn and at which Harry works, bending over his papers and walking round and round the table from one task to the next, talking into his dictating machine. Somebody once said it looked like a wartime operations room, and in a way that describes it exactly.

Just when, at last, I thought I had him talking seriously about himself, he launches into the story of how he went blind in his right eye during the 1983 ABTA conference in Palma. But he tells the story in such a matter-of-fact way that we both end up laughing about the way events unfolded.

He woke in his Palma hotel room to find he could not see with his right eye and, assuming it was the same kind of problem he had experienced with his left eye six years earlier, telephoned the surgeon in London who had performed those earlier operations. Ordered to fly home immediately, he was examined by that surgeon who said, in Harry's words: 'I'm delighted to tell you it is not a detached retina, just a haemorrhage'. 'Just a haemorrhage' would have been enough to floor most people, but Harry took the surgeon's advice to leave well alone in the hope that it would disperse after a few months. Six months later he returned to the consulting rooms, still without the sight of his right eye. 'The surgeon examined me and said: "Good God, now you have got a detached retina. You must come in for an operation immediately!" So I went in,' explains Harry ruefully, 'and that was that.'

And he laughs at his six eyes – the pair God gave him, plus contact lenses, plus spectacles. From time to time he has to put on his black eyepatch, and those in the travel trade who have long regarded him as a bit of a buccaneer think this is highly appropriate.

But what about the trappings of success? One is always fascinated by the evidence of a person's fortune in life. By 1970 both Harry and Rene realised that they were earning well and were, moreover, worth a good deal. 'We decided we'd spent some of that money. We bought a Jensen, although we already had a Jaguar. We bought that flat, which is now worth half a million or more, and we bought the new boat.' He has already told the story of how he bought his Park Lane penthouse and his first boat, and even that Jensen which cost him £8,000 back in 1970 – a considerable sum for what he was once forced to describe as 'a mobile rat's nest'.

Also in 1970 he bought a new boat to replace the one he had bought in the year of his son Peter's death – the boat he had bought back from Poole with the aid of a road atlas and an incredible amount of beginner's luck. 'We brought it through the Goodwin Sands in the night, with the place looking like Piccadilly Circus with all those red and green lights,' he says. 'We didn't know what any of the lights meant and how we ever got it home I'll never know.'

'The new boat we got cheap,' he confesses. Harry is full of confessions like that. 'We paid £18,000 for it, having seen it when it was half built. Robin Knox-Johnson was running the boatyard and asked if he could exhibit it at the Boat Show before handing it over to us. Promising to hold it at that price and throw in a few extras afterwards.'

Robin was as good as his word, although by the time the Boat Show came along, six months later, the price tag was £25,000. How much is it worth today? Harry doesn't know. 'It's a forty-footer, and they used to say boats cost £1,000 a foot, so I suppose it's worth a lot more than we paid for it,' he smiles.

Right, Harry Chandler, is there a secret to your success? The question is inevitable, although I do not think Harry Chandler has any secret apart from an application of hard work and a modicum of luck. And an ability to see and sieze opportunities. He talks about the important decisions he and Rene have made which turned out right – the decision to return to the business after the war, the decision to sell direct to the public rather than go through travel agents, the decision to concentrate on the Algarve region of Portugal when Rene 'discovered' it, and the decision to keep the business to a size where they can both know what is going on. 'Our business isn't complicated, and we both see it in simple terms of black and white,' he told me. 'I'm glad we stayed fairly small because I'm not an organisation man. I like it best when Rene and I can sort things out together.'

That he relies a great deal on his wife is obvious to anyone who knows him – or, rather, who knows the pair of them. She often appears to despair of his antics, of the statements he makes to the travel trade press, of the stands he takes on business issues and the fact that he goes straight for an objective without regard to the finer feelings of those who might inadvertently be standing in the way.

To hear Rene's plaintive cry of 'Oh, Harry', when he cheerfully puts his foot in it, is to hear the cry of wives down the ages whose husbands are sometimes too much to handle. What he would do without her indeed, what they would do without each other – I hate to think.

But underneath it all, underneath the Cockney sparrow exterior of a lad who had ideas above his station, the rock bottom, rock solid base of Harry Chandler is a plain honesty which members of his trade have come to recognise and respect – albeit reluctantly on the part of some. Whether they agree with him or not – and plenty do not – nobody doubts his sincerity. Which is why he has been so successful in the role of honest broker, or backstage statesman. It was in that role that he became involved in the aftermath of the Laker collapse in 1982, an event which tested loyalties and friendships all round the trade.

'The eight directors of the TOSG trust fund are personally liable for misuse of the fund's money,' he told me in the upstairs office. 'That's why we had to get that indemnity from Peter Shore in 1974. And that's why we are very sensitive to what is right and what is wrong. We were somewhat suspicious of the Laker situation and in August of 1981 we asked George Carroll if we could see the accounts.'

The situation was a delicate one, for George Carroll, managing director of the Laker travel company, was at that time chairman of the trust fund. A man whose personal honour could not be doubted.

'In September or October of 1981, George showed us the accounts for the year ended the previous April and they looked satisfactory, with healthy profits. George also told us bookings were looking good. We accepted what we were shown, but the Trust Fund Lawyer, Harvey Crush, asked if there were any cross guarantees between the two tour operating companies (Laker and Arrowsmith) and the airline, and George Carroll agreed to ask Sir Freddie Laker whether such information could be made available to us. We continued to press for this information, right up to the morning of February 5th, 1982, when we were told that there were, indeed, very heavy cross guarantees. The Clydesdale Bank had that very morning called upon both tour operating companies to pay more than £14 million, which of course they could not do and all the companies went into liquidation. We subsequently found that cash received from holidaymakers by the two tour operating companies was instantly passed to the parent airline to keep it flying, and that cash had of course disappeared,' Harry told me.

When Laker collapsed, TOSG moved once more to effect a rescue of stranded passengers and to deal with the claims of those who had paid for winter and summer holidays. Some 52,000 claims were met from the Laker bond and ATRF coffers, but the aftermath of Laker lingers on, as does a degree of dissention at the part played by the banks and credit card companies who are still in dispute with Travel Agents who have claims against Barclaycard still unpaid, for holidays they provided for Laker clients.

Looking at the state of the travel trade in the 1980s, Harry Chandler says most of its troubles stem from excess capacity – too many holidays chasing too few customers. That, and the tendency of tour companies to dump unsold holidays on the market at cheap prices.

'Because they've been doing this, people have been hanging back before making their bookings and paying their deposits,' he explains. 'This deprives the tour operator of his main source of income, that important early cash. What many people in the business have failed to realise is that tour operators should really be doing three basic things. First, selling holidays. Now you don't have to make a profit on that part of your business – just break even. Second, acting as bankers by investing that early cash flow, and that is where the main source of profit lies. Third, gambling on the foreign exchange markets, again making profits if we know from our experience how currencies are likely to move.'

In his view those factors never change, no matter what fads or fancies affect business year to year. He also believes, as I happen to believe, that the travel trade's endearing optimism is one of its most pleasant yet most dangerous characteristics. Year after year the holiday companies bring out their new catalogues, their sales brochures filled with dreams and promises. Dreams and promises are all they have to sell, welded on to the factual base of aircraft seats and hotel beds. And year after year they believe they will succeed individually even if all rivals fail. Behind the scenes they may worry about the state of the economy or the value of the pound, they may know that short time working means less money put aside for next summer's holiday, they may wrestle with rising prices around the Mediterranean and farther afield. But because they are selling dreams and promises, they have to ignore all that and hope the rest of us will ignore it also.

In spite of all that – or maybe even because of all that – the holiday business holds a fascination for anyone who observes it, or who becomes involved in it.

'It's a good business to be in,' Harry says. 'It's good because it enables me to earn a decent living, if you want to look at it from that simple point of view. But it's also good because it provides employment for people in other countries, many of whom have nothing much else apart from tourism to rely on. It gives people the chance to live differently – better, I hope – for a couple of weeks a year, maybe more. It can be a tremendous force for good in a world that's seen too much of war and evil. I'm glad I'm in it. I'm glad I made the decision to go into it, back in 1936.'

Oh yes, that was another of Harry Chandler's good decisions – to become 'A holiday tour organiser'. His father didn't much like the idea. For one thing it meant taking people to Germany and, in common with many of his generation, he hated the Germans. He had also pulled a few strings and was able to offer young Harry a proper job as a tram conductor in Canning Town at £2.10s a week. And there was a pension at 65.

'I was 20 years old then. What did I care about the prospect of a pension at 65?' says Harry with an expansive grin.

I do not think he cares much about the prospect of a pension even now.

CHAPTER 14

Future Trends

TO WHERE will it go from here, the story of Harry Chandler, and of Rene and their son Paul, and of The Travel Club of Upminster? Should I try to do a little crystal gazing, or – better still – rely on past experience to fashion my assessment of the future?

In the first place, as long as Harry and Rene control the business, I see no reason why it should alter its basic pattern of size. Kept at around 35,000 passengers a year with a turnover exceeding £10 million a year, it is an operation that can be overseen by the pair of them and whose quality can be controlled. Though they have an excellent staff at Upminster (and are the very first to admit how much they depend on them), Harry and Rene Chandler have made a success of their business because they are able to have a personal influence on every aspect of it – to the extent that they have done away with the 'small print' brochure conditions in their dealings with the public and rely on common sense and common law to see them through. The Travel Club has an enviable record as far as its customer relations are concerned, because there is a kind of rapport between the company and its clients. So much so that, when faced with a rare complaining letter some years ago, Harry Chandler investigated the situation personally, decided there was no fault to be found, and wrote to the customer in very sharp terms. The Travel Club was constantly seeking to improve its service, he pointed out, and also seeking to improve the quality of its clientele. As the complainant did not come up to standard, The Travel Club would no longer be prepared to take him on holiday. Game, set and match.

Because the company has not introduced any new destinations for some years, it can concentrate on improving, year by year, those holidays it does offer. This has resulted in a very high volume of repeat bookings and, in an industry that is selling an intangible product, that kind of goodwill is invaluable. The Chandlers do not want to increase their share of the market and so can rely on getting the right number of people on to their aircraft – that vitally important 'load factor'. Because of this, The Travel Club remained unaffected by the turmoil at the beginning of 1985 when tour companies were forced to amalgamate their flights and other arrangements and so upset the plans of many thousands of their customers. The travel trade falls back too easily on this 'consolidation' option having failed to get the sums right in the first place, but it is an option that leaves a sour taste in the mouths of their customers. Illwill rather than goodwill.

One of the other benefits the Chandlers enjoy is that they need not spend a fortune on advertising. They deal direct with the public, so no 'middle man' travel agent has to be wooed and won. It is a comfortable state of affairs.

But it can not last for ever. Harry and Rene are not, to use Harry's phrase, 'in the first flush of youth', and some day the business will no longer be under their control. Which is where Paul Chandler comes in, although when I spoke to him I very soon realised this was not a question of a favoured son being handed his parents' business on a plate. In the first place, his early years were spent demonstrating that he neither wanted nor needed an involvement in the business but was determined to carve his own route to the top.

That determination took him from Essex University (sociology and computer science) to Switzerland, Algeria and South America. He had, in fact, expected to go on to Cardiff University to study town planning but when the promised place there was no longer available, he found himself at a loose end in London.

He took an intensive course at International House in Shaftesbury Avenue to obtain the qualifications needed to teach English as a second language – 'one of our greatest exports is the English language' – and set off to do just that. In Switzerland there were 11 different nationalities in his class. He also worked, he told me, in a girls' finishing school, confessing that he got fired from that enviable job. Why? 'We'll draw a veil over that.'

From Switzerland he moved to Algeria to work in an oil refinery. Together with Ursula, a girl he had met at Essex, he worked also in South America before returning to England to attend the London College of Printing. Starting up a printing and pottery business came next, the location being Helensburgh in Scotland. It went well, and is still going well under the direction of his original partner, but Paul had to pull out, mainly because of a desire to try something else, and partly because Ursula flatly refused to live north of the Border.

'We ended up drawing a ring around London, indicating three hours' driving distance. I wouldn't live closer and Ursula wouldn't go any further,' he told me. 'The line came through Worcestershire and when we came here to look around we bought the first place we saw, a redundant hop kiln at Suckley. It's a listed building and quite a responsibility, but we realised we could make it work for us.'

The couple married and Ursula now runs the pottery business they founded in the old kiln. It was when Harry had his first heart attack in 1977 that Paul began to think he might have a contribution to make to

The Travel Club. 'I thought about what would happen to the business when my parents retired – as we euphemistically put it. It could be destroyed. Not because the staff would not be able to control it, but because there would be tremendous pressure for it to be absolved by other, bigger firms.'

Knowing that the basis of The Travel Club is the goodwill it enjoys, and that it also has a responsibility to a lot of people overseas – the small hotels, for instance, which rely on the company to fill their rooms each summer – Paul Chandler thought long and hard.

At the same time, and by coincidence, Harry and Rene were being persuaded, mainly by their staff, that the firm should get into the computer age and make use of the kind of technology that was proving essential to many others in the industry. They agreed that Paul's experience should be employed, so he began to look over the kind of systems that were available to small businesses. Obviously The Travel Club would have to start with something small and feel its way through the computer jungle. 'I became much involved in this, putting in a lot of time writing computer programmes, which is a sure fire way to learn about the business. I didn't like anything I saw in the computer field, so I devised a system for us,' he explained.

During the course of this, he realised that the company needed a second generation Chandler, and is now enthusiastically involved as a director. However, the work he put in on computers gave him the experience to set up as a computer consultant and, with a partner, is doing well in that field from a base in Malvern.

As if The Travel Club, the Pottery and the computer consultancy were, not enough, Paul took a keen interest in politics, becoming a member of the local authority and being adopted by the Liberal/SDP Alliance as prospective candidate for Malvern and South Worcestershire.

At the time of writing, that constituency is regarded as a two horse race between the Liberal/SDP and the Conservatives. The sitting member is Michael Spicer, Minister of Aviation and Paul Chandler would need to get an eight per cent swing to capture the seat. Perhaps that cannot be achieved in one General Election, but it is possible over two. Should that happen, and the Chandlers end up with an MP in the family, we are into a whole new ball game. . .

That could be part of the scenario over the next ten years, but in the meantime Paul Chandler is an active ingredient in the future of The Travel Club. Having had a childhood dominated by the business, he knows enough to avoid the mistakes of over-ambition. And at 35 he has the maturity to appreciate the solid, old-fashioned values upon which his parents have built up their business.

But let me not run on too long in this vein, for I can almost hear Harry and Rene reminding me that they are not out of the picture by any means. And of course they are not, but when you are trying to assess the future, you have to take all possibilities into consideration. So let me change tack a little and think about the kind of general changes The Travel Club will experience – changes in the environment of the industry, in business patterns and practices.

The way things are shaping, the giants of the travel trade – the likes of Thomson Holidays, Intasun and maybe three or four others – will get bigger. I do not believe they will all survive, for tour operating demands a lot of up-front investment and entails a fair amount of risk. Those in ultimate control of large companies may decide they could do better investing their money, time and effort elsewhere. Where does that leave the small companies, such as The Travel Club? It leaves them, in my view, having to stay small and concentrate on those things they each do best. Providing 'special interest' holidays, for example. Holidays aimed at smallish sections of the public who will do business only with firms which are seen to recognise their particular needs, whether those small sections have sporting or hobby interests, are keen on music festivals, gardening tours, pilgrimages and the like. It is not worth the big boys' time to cultivate those special sections, to become involved in their little worlds and achieve a high profile – big fish in a small pond, if you like. But, if they want to stay in business, the minor league tour operators will head in that direction. They could also achieve the same effect by appealing to the general public as specialist operators to a particular country. In a way, The Travel Club has already done this with its programme of holidays to the Algarve.

What new holiday areas could be exploited in the way the Algarve was in the 1960s? Harry Chandler and I recently tried to compile a list of locations, and agreed that places farther away are likely to become more popular – islands in the Indian Ocean, Hong Kong, Bangkok, Singapore and the Philippines. India and Australia, too, could receive many more tourists from the UK. There is little likelihood that a 200-mile stretch of coastline, comparable with the Algarve of 20 years ago, will ever be found within 1500 miles of UK airports, but there is one south-facing Mediterranean coastline that is hardly developed, that has the beaches to attract tourists and whose government and people are interested in the economic benefits that tourism could bring. This is the southern coast of Turkey, and when I have talked to Harry Chandler about it, I think (only think, mind you) that I have caught a gleam in his eye. Will that south coast be the Algarve of the 80s and 90s? And if it is, will The Travel Club be in there promoting it? That is something the crystal ball will not tell me.

But what I can see in the past is that, back in the 1950s and early 1960s, the big boys of the British travel trade became very complacent and that complacency led to all sorts of problems for them and for their customers. That must not happen again, which is why there is a need for independent characters like Harry Chandler to stay around.

Which means the industry will need plenty of people who can resist the 'benefits of scale' argument, deployed to justify expansion upon expansion. There will be plenty who will go along the expansionist path, aiming for an annual market of 200,000 customers or thereabouts, employing expensive technology and batteries of experts in a bid to become a household name – another Thomson, if you like. Against such expansionists the trade, and the holidaymaking public, will need the travel industry's equivalent of the corner shop – the operator who is happy with his 30,000 or 40,000 customers, who can keep a personal touch in his dealings with them, and who can afford to offer the kind of choice or special arrangements that the giants disregard. Human nature will see to it that such mavericks exist, and that their instinct will be to question the way the trade does business, just as Harry Chandler has questioned and argued and fought for all those fifty years.

What they think of Harry

SID SILVER – veteran tour operator, former boss of Cosmos
'I have mixed views on his influence on events, for he has obviously had various axes to grind. I differ from him on "Stabiliser" and some other issues, but he wants to keep his freedom to be an independent voice, away from the galloping herd. I respect him for that. He keeps debate going, and is a most convincing spokesman for tour operators and the travel trade generally.'

Gordon McNally – chairman, Exchange Travel
'We have clashed on various items. As president of TOSG he was the fall guy. When the tour operators had nasty things to say or do to the travel agents they had to have a front man who wouldn't be penalised for saying it. So they popped Harry up front.'

Vladimir Raitz – tour operator, former boss of Horizon
'I've known him for many years. I'm very fond of him and he's one of the nicest people in the business. Obviously some people hate him because of his non-agent policy. But we are old friends.'

Cliff Jones – outspoken retail agent
'We've locked horns on countless occasions and done battle in councils, and so on. But the beauty of it is that we can come out of the room, put our arms round each other's shoulders, and go off and have a drink. He is, sadly, one of the few "characters" left in the industry. Whether you agreed with him or not, he has stood by what he said, and said it fearlessly.'

Colin Collins – former Editor *Travel Trade Gazette*, PRO for Clarksons, now publisher of *Travelnews*
'One of the most canny businessmen I've met, with an inbuilt ability to get on and do things which corporate heirarchies taken months even to

consider. As a publicist, he could give lessons; as a diplomat, he could sometimes use them; as a friend, he's been tremendous; as a competitor, downright annoying.'

Michael Barratt – Television personality

For integrity and true personal involvement – *caring* for the people they take on holiday – Harry and Rene Chandler are unique in the travel industry. Their clients become their friends, which surely says it all!

Jill Crawshaw – Travel Editor, *Standard*

What I like most about Harry Chandler is that he gives it to you straight – the not-always-palateable truth. While other tour operators are busy telling you what a marvellous season they're having, Harry will tell you it is absolutely catastrophic. He's always honest.

Elisabeth de Stroumillo – Travel writer, *Daily Telegraph*

I love him dearly. He was one of the first people I met when I took up travel journalism. I've always found him astringent and worth listening to, even when he was talking through the back of his head, because there was always the germ of an idea somewhere. He's very approachable and willing to sound off on any subject, which is lovely if you need somebody to fill in the background or give you an iconoclastic opinion.

Roger Bray – air and travel correspondent, *Standard*

He's been a maverick, but at the same time he's been a catalyst in the industry. In spite of not having one of the biggest operations in the country – far from it – he's consistently been at the forefront of every controversy. One of the nice things about Harry is that he is never over-diplomatic and always prepared to call a spade a spade.

Arthur Sandles – Leisure Editor, *Financial Times*

Your first impression of Harry Chandler is one of a likeable rogue. After twenty years, that impression remains. An absolute charmer who would not willingly cause pain to anyone, he has that enviable knack of making you think he has done you a favour by giving him a good deal. His secret is his hard-nosed naivity – fascinated by everything and anything, but with a sixth sense to protect himself against a wrong move. He's a bit of a mix between innocent kitten and jungle wise jaguar.

A View from Albert Goring

ST CLEER is a small village in Cornwall, on the south-eastern corner of Bodmin Moor. If you drive into it from the direction of Liskeard, some two miles away, and turn right at the post office, then right again, you will find yourself at the entrance gate of a small development of houses built in the mid-1970s. In one of those houses lives Albert Goring, the man who shared those cycling adventures with young Harry Chandler, who went with him on those first trips to Germany, and who helped him compile his early 'brochures'. It was in 1976 that Albert Goring came to live in St. Cleer with his second wife Jill, when he retired from the library service.

In his upstairs study with views out over the moors towards Caradon Hill, Albert Goring ponders over the fact that Harry Chandler regarded him as 'the intellectual one', and an early influence on his life.

'I don't think anyone influenced Harry Chandler very much,' he says. 'Though I haven't seen much of him and Rene in recent years, I do know that she's had to fight all her life not to be submerged! In the early days he was something of a steamroller. You had to keep your end up and fire as good as you got, or you would disappear under the weight of his enthusiasm for some scheme or other.'

Albert, who is six months older, met Harry first when they were about 13 years old and went together to the Grove School. Scholarship pupils, they ended up in the same class and though Albert Goring was not a model pupil, he took more interest in his studies than young Harry. 'He wasn't interested in school work at all. He just did the minimum to get by and sculled about at the bottom of the class. I was usually up near the top, and I always seemed to be getting into hot water, whereas Harry got away with it. He had a lot of likeable qualities about him, and the masters accepted his academic failings because of this.'

When the two boys left school Harry took the London Chamber of Commerce examination and joined Continental Express. Albert answered an advertisement for a job in the local library. 'I decided perhaps that this was for me, a nice safe job' and beat thirty other candidates to get it. 'I studied to become qualified as a librarian, went to

University College and took a library course, and stayed in that job until I went into the RAF in 1940, 'he explains. Beginning as a fitter, he qualified as an aircrew member, first with Coastal Command and later with Transport Command. 'I married in 1945 and thought for a while of staying in the RAF, but in the end I went back to my library career,' he says. 'I stayed in West Ham for about a year, then got a job in Wandsworth. That was a really big move – south of the river! Though I made various attempts to get jobs in other parts of the country, I never succeeded, and remained in Wandsworth. In the end I became a district librarian, in charge of a number of libraries, and that's what I was doing when I retired in 1976.'

Albert Goring is tall and spare; any tendency to 'bookishness' as a result of his librarian years is balanced by a wry and gentle sense of humour.

He recalls his and Harry's years of studying at evening classes and cycling adventures which came to an end with Harry's transfer to Bradford. But their friendship remained and their adventures resumed with that first trip to Germany in 1934.

'I may have been a bit sceptical about foreign travel. Certainly I needed to be persuaded,' he says. 'I wanted to go, but I thought there were more complications than Harry foresaw. It was a time, don't forget, when Hitler had just taken over as Chancellor and there was lots of unrest in Germany.'

We talk about those pre-war trips by bike and by tandem and how Harry came to realise that he could organise holidays at a price which the ordinary clerk or the better paid manual worker could afford. 'Working people, then, never considered going abroad. That was for the middle and professional classes. They went with Cooks or had villas they rented regularly. But the manual and clerical workers never thought they could afford it. But the Workers' Travel Association, Polytechnic Travel, and then Harry Chandler showed them they could.'

Would he have been interested in joining Harry in creating what was to become The Travel Club? Albert Goring is certain on that point – he is not, nor was then the 'outgoing' type, so it would not have suited him. 'I could have done the office work, I suppose, but he didn't need anybody to do that. And of course, later on, Rene took over that side of things.'

'She constantly had to keep her end up with Harry and people, especially women, might have felt she was aggressive. She thought that Londoners were rather jumped up and bumptious and who regarded Northerners as clots. But she was an outgoing person who got on well with people. There might have been stormy periods in their marriage, but it is certainly the case that Rene didn't intend to let Harry steamroller her and use her as a convenient person to run his office. I am sure that, being a forceful personality, she has been of great benefit to him socially.'

He recalls some of the schemes Harry tried out in order to make money during the winters of those years before the war – his involvement

with the lady who had an infallible system for winning at roulette, his attempt to sell sandpaper to furniture makers in Hackney, and his investment in the 'travel agency' that went broke after a couple of weeks.
attempt to sell sandpaper to furniture makers in Hackney, his investment in the 'travel agency' that went broke after a couple of weeks and his venture into pin tables in East End cafés, debt collecting for the radio shop, and portering at the GPO.

'I used to write his prospectus for him, up until the war,' Albert Goring recalls. 'I did it as a favour for a friend. But, do you know, I never went on one of his holidays until 1982 when my wife and I went to Majorca. It was the first time I'd ever been there and I quite enjoyed it.'

Index

Malvern, 158
Marbella, 131
Marseilles, 121
Mason, Roy, 141
Mediterranean, 78, 121, 123, 159
Menton, 108, 122
MI5, 65, 66–78
Middleton, Roy, 118–20
Montechoro, 127
Mountbatten, Lord, 85–7
Munich, 31

Nazis, 32, 95–6
Needles, 118, 120
Newhaven, 104
Nice, 111–12

Oberammergau, 108
Omar Khayyam Tours, 141
Operation Stabiliser, 141–3
Ostend, 38, 43, 104

Palestine, 73, 76
Paris, 108, 121
Park Lane penthouse, 133–4, 147, 151
Penang, 85, 90
Penina golf course, 130–1
Perez, Sydney, 109
Perpignan, 111–12, 140
Philippines, 159
Pickfords, 82, 146
Poland, 47–8
Polytechnic Touring Association, 47, 164
Pontetressa, 107
Poole, 117–18, 122, 153
Portugal, 124–5, 128–31, 133
Praia da Rocha, 126
Preston, 80–3
Public Speaking, 21

Raitz, Vladimir, 109–10, 145, 161
Ramsgate, 119
Rangoon, 85, 90
Restrictive Practises Court, 142
Russell School, 39

Sadgunn, Edgar, 141
Saga Holidays, 127
Sagres, 126
St James's flat, 133–4
Sarnen, 40, 44–6, 48–50, 97, 103–5, 107
Schwangau, 33–4, 37–9
Scotland, 20, 69
Sea Princess, 76–7
Seefeld, 32, 33, 108, 111
Sete, 121
Shore, Peter, 147–9, 154
Sicily, 72–3, 147

Silver, Sid, 161
Simpson, Lieut-Gen, 93
Sinai Desert, 73
Singapore, 85–91, 92–3, 104, 159
Skelton, George, 82–3, 89, 146–7
Smyrck, Bob, 83
South Africa, 70
Southend, 115, 116
Spain, 125, 148–9
Springfield Court, 59, 93, 97
Stella boat, 122
Stephen's Road, 15, 22
Strasbourg, 48
Suckley, 157
Suez, 72, 83
Swissair, 109, 110
Swiss Bank Corporation, 144
Switzerland, 33, 39, 40, 46, 47–52, 56, 97–8, 101, 104–7, 133, 157

Tebbit, Norman, 149
Tel Aviv, 74–5
Telegraph and Argus, 23
Templer, Gen Sir Gerald, 93
Tenerife, 133
The Spectator, 107
The Times, 34
Thomson Holidays, 145, 159–60
Three Passes Tour, 45
Tobruk, 68
Tour Operators Council, 142
Tour Operators Study Group, 128, 142–50, 152, 154
Townend, Paul, 46
Travel Club of Upminster, 11–12, 108, 129, 132–3, 156–60, 164
Turkey, 159

Upminster, 12, 31, 59, 79–80, 93, 98, 103, 107, 116, 121, 124, 133, 146, 149, 151–2

Vale do Lobo, 10, 136
Victoria Station, 19, 47, 98, 100, 104

Wales, 20
Weavers Down, 83
Wedgwood Benn, Antony, 146, 149–50
Weggis, 107
West Ham, 15–16, 22
Williams, Mrs, 23
Winchester, 20, 66
Workers' Travel Association, 33, 47, 109, 164
World War I, 15, 23, 25, 32
World War II, 11, 16, 49–54
WVS, 75, 89–91, 93

YMCA, 19
YWCA Singapore, 92